Easy to Use, Easy to Carry
One Chord on Every Page

Jake Jackson

FLAME TREE
PUBLISHING

Publisher & Creative Director: Nick Wells
Editor: Polly Prior
Designer and diagrams: Jake

Special thanks to Laura Bulbeck, Sara Robson and Catherine Taylor

This edition published in 2011
First edition published in 2006 (10:22)

16 18 20 19 17
11 13 15 17 19 18 16 14 12

This edition first published 2011 by
FLAME TREE PUBLISHING
6 Melbray Mews
Fulham, London SW6 3NS
United Kingdom
www.flametreepublishing.com

Music website: www.flametreemusic.com

ISBN 978-0-85775-263-5

A CIP record for this book is available from the
British Library upon request.

Acknowledgements
All images and notation © copyright **Foundry Arts** 2011

Jake Jackson is a musician and writer of practical music books. His publications include *Advanced Guitar Chords*; *Beginner's Guide to Reading Music; Chords for Kids*; *Classic Riffs*; *Guitar Chords*; *How to Play Electric Guitar*; *Piano and Keyboard Chords*; *Scales and Modes* and *The Songwriter's Rhyming Dictionary.*

Printed in China

Contents

Guitar Chords is divided into keys, which are easily accessible using the **tabs** along the edge of the page, with **one chord per page**. Each chord is offered with the **first** and **second position**, giving you more than enough to play along with any popular song, or jam with others in a band setting.

Use the tabs on the side of each page to find the chord you want quickly.

At the end of the book you'll find some more advanced chords, with four on each page.

Individual notes that make up the chord.

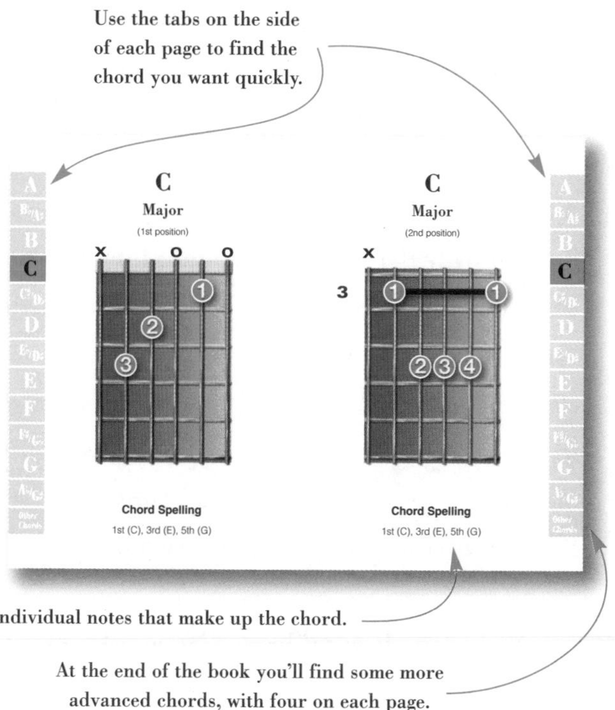

How to Use the Chord Boxes

The chord fretboxes in this book will help you to learn the shapes of hundreds of chords, and will be a useful reference guide when you are playing and composing your own music. This is by no means a comprehensive manual, but it should serve as a handy reminder to even the most adventurous guitarists.

- While it might seem dull learning the fingerings, remember that the **wider** your **chord vocabulary** becomes, the more you will be able to vary your playing style and compositions. It is particularly important to know your chords if you are planning to jam with other musicians – when someone shouts out 'E!', you don't want to be left high and dry wondering where the chord might be while the other musicians sail off into the next verse.

- The chords are **divided** by **key**, from A to G♯ (A♭), with the key's notes shown at the top of the page.

- Each chord is shown with **two different fingerings** or **positions**. Technically, there are at least four fingerings for each chord and some have many more, but this can become confusing, so, in order to include a greater variety of chords and to make this book easy to use, we have restricted ourselves to two chord positions only.

- The **left-hand** pages outline the main chords you will need to learn. These are chords in the **first position**.

- The **right-hand** pages offer chords in the **second position**. These can be useful especially when fitting them into a progression – when you are playing in higher fingerboard positions, you do not want to have to stop and scrabble around trying to find a chord position back on the first few frets.

- The diagrams throughout show the guitar **fretboard** in an **upright** position, with **high E** on the **right**. The **nut** appears at the top if the chord is played on the lower frets.

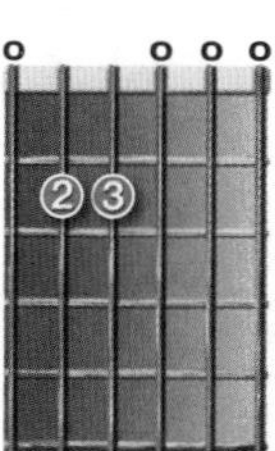

- If the chord is in a higher position, the **fret number** on which it begins is given to the left of the diagram.

- The notes to be played are shown as circles, with the finger number that should be used for each note:

① = index finger	② = middle finger	③ = ring finger	④ = little finger

An **X** above the string shows that the string should **not** be played. An **O** above the string shows that it should be played as an **open string**.

- We have tried to make the chord presentation as easy to use as possible, so where there is a choice of note name (e.g. F♯ or G♭) we have selected the one that you are most likely to come across in your playing.

- Where a chord contains a **flattened** (♭) or **sharpened** (♯) interval (e.g. ♯5th), you can find the notes by playing a fret **lower** (for a **flat**) or a fret **higher** (for a **sharp**) than the interval note indicated at the top of the page. In the keys that contain a large number of sharps or flats, double flats (𝄫) and double sharps (x) sometimes occur in the augmented and diminished chords. A double flat is the note two frets below the named note, while a double sharp is two frets up.

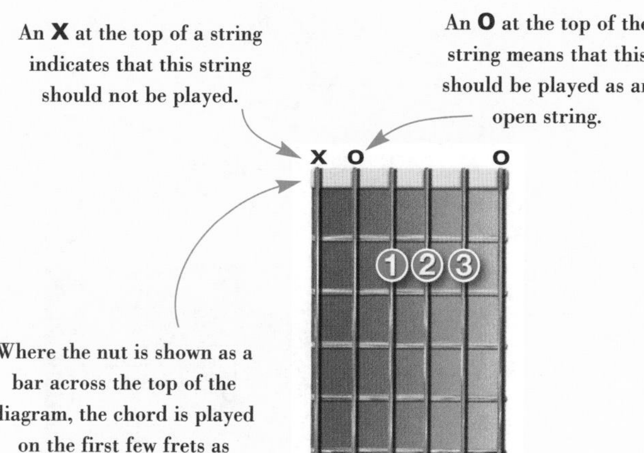
An **X** at the top of a string indicates that this string should not be played.
An **O** at the top of the string means that this should be played as an open string.
X O O
1 2 3
Where the nut is shown as a bar across the top of the diagram, the chord is played on the first few frets as shown in relation to the nut.

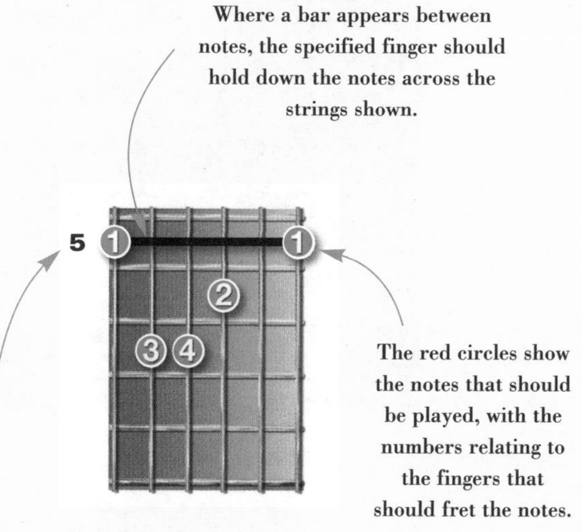
Where a bar appears between notes, the specified finger should hold down the notes across the strings shown.
5
1 1
2
3 4
The red circles show the notes that should be played, with the numbers relating to the fingers that should fret the notes.
Where the chord is to be played higher up the fretboard, the fret number is shown to the left of the diagram.

A

Major

(1st position)

Chord Spelling

1st (A), 3rd (C♯), 5th (E)

A

Major

(2nd position)

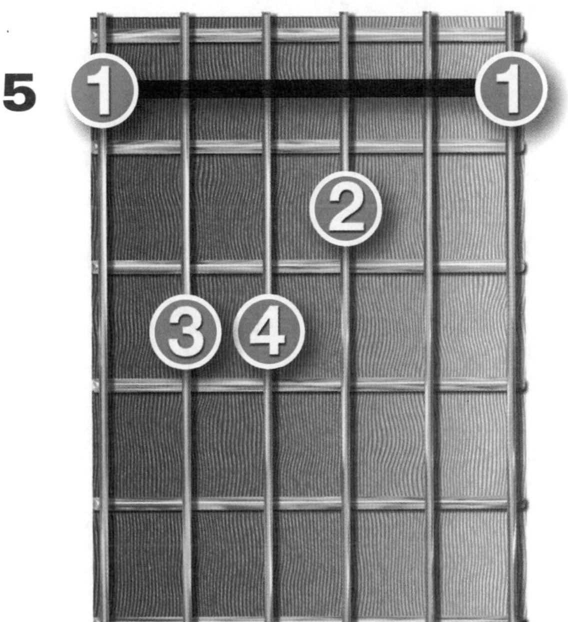

Chord Spelling

1st (A), 3rd (C♯), 5th (E)

A
B♭/A♯
B
C
C♯/D♭
D
E♭/D♯
E
F
F♯/G♭
G
A♭/G♯
Other Chords

Am

Minor

(1st position)

Chord Spelling

1st (A), ♭3rd (C), 5th (E)

Am

Minor

(2nd position)

Chord Spelling

1st (A), ♭3rd (C), 5th (E)

Amaj7

Major 7th

(1st position)

Chord Spelling

1st (A), 3rd (C♯), 5th (E), 7th (G♯)

Amaj7

Major 7th

(2nd position)

4

Chord Spelling

1st (A), 3rd (C♯), 5th (E), 7th (G♯)

A
B♭/A♯
B
C
C♯/D♭
D
E♭/D♯
E
F
F♯/G♭
G
A♭/G♯
Other Chords

Am7

Minor 7th

(1st position)

Chord Spelling

1st (A), ♭3rd (C), 5th (E), ♭7th (G)

Am7

Minor 7th

(2nd position)

Chord Spelling

1st (A), ♭3rd (C), 5th (E), ♭7th (G)

Asus4

Suspended 4th

(1st position)

Chord Spelling

1st (A), 4th (D), 5th (E)

Asus4

Suspended 4th

(2nd position)

X O

5

Chord Spelling

1st (A), 4th (D), 5th (E)

A7sus4

Dominant 7th Suspended 4th

(1st position)

Chord Spelling

1st (A), 4th (D), 5th (E), ♭7th (G)

A7sus4

Dominant 7th Suspended 4th

(2nd position)

Chord Spelling

1st (A), 4th (D), 5th (E), ♭7th (G)

A6

Major 6th

(1st position)

Chord Spelling

1st (A), 3rd (C♯), 5th (E), 6th (F♯)

A6

Major 6th

(2nd position)

4

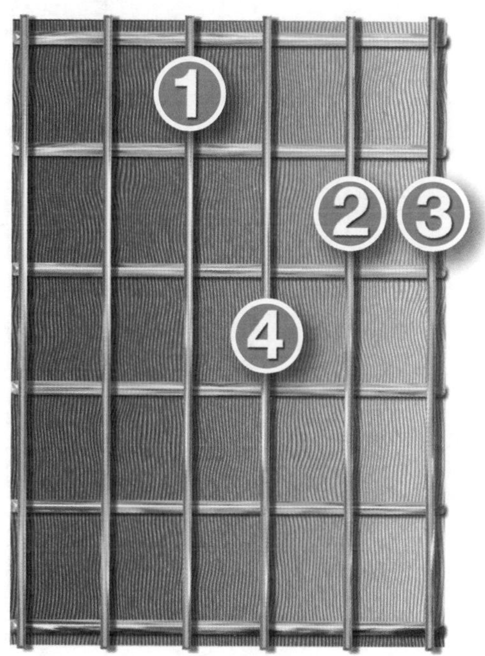

Chord Spelling

1st (A), 3rd (C♯), 5th (E), 6th (F♯)

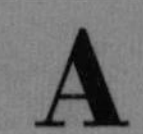

Am6

Minor 6th

(1st position)

Chord Spelling

1st (A), ♭3rd (C), 5th (E), 6th (F♯)

Am6

Minor 6th

(2nd position)

Chord Spelling

1st (A), ♭3rd (C), 5th (E), 6th (F♯)

A
B♭/A♯
B
C
C♯/D♭
D
E♭/D♯
E
F
F♯/G♭
G
A♭/G♯
Other Chords

A
B♭/A♯
B
C
C♯/D♭
D
E♭/D♯
E
F
F♯/G♭
G
A♭/G♯
Other Chords

A7

Dominant 7th

(1st position)

Chord Spelling

1st (A), 3rd (C♯), 5th (E), ♭7th (G)

A7

Dominant 7th

(2nd position)

Chord Spelling

1st (A), 3rd (C♯), 5th (E), ♭7th (G)

A
B♭/A♯
B
C
C♯/D♭
D
E♭/D♯
E
F
F♯/G♭
G
A♭/G♯
Other Chords

A9

Dominant 9th

(1st position)

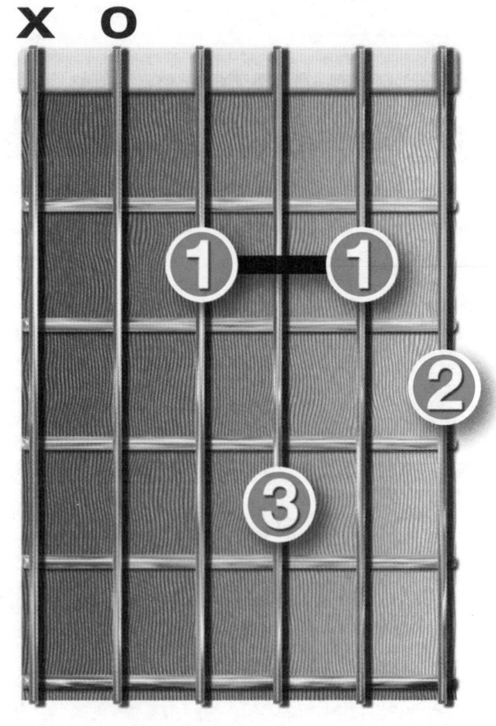

Chord Spelling

1st (A), 3rd (C♯), 5th (E), ♭7th (G), 9th (B)

A9

Dominant 9th

(2nd position)

4

Chord Spelling

1st (A), 3rd (C♯), 5th (E), ♭7th (G), 9th (B)

A
B♭/A♯
B
C
C♯/D♭
D
E♭/D♯
E
F
F♯/G♭
G
A♭/G♯
Other Chords

A5

5th 'Power Chord'

(1st position)

Chord Spelling

1st (A), 5th (E)

A6add9

Major 6th add 9th

(1st position)

Chord Spelling

1st (A), 3rd (C♯), 5th (E), 6th (F♯), 9th (B)

A11

Dominant 11th

(1st position)

3

Chord Spelling

1st (A), 3rd (C♯), 5th (E), ♭7th (G), 9th (B), 11th (D)

A13

Dominant 13th

(1st position)

X O

2

Chord Spelling

1st (A), 3rd (C♯), 5th (E), ♭7th (G),
9th (B), 11th (D), 13th (F♯)

A
B♭/A♯
B
C
C♯/D♭
D
E♭/D♯
E
F
F♯/G♭
G
A♭/G♯
Other Chords

Aadd9

Major add 9th

(1st position)

Chord Spelling

1st (A), 3rd (C♯), 5th (E), 9th (B)

Am9

Minor 9th

(1st position)

Chord Spelling

1st (A), ♭3rd (C), 5th (E), ♭7th (G),
9th (B)

Amaj9

Major 9th

(1st position)

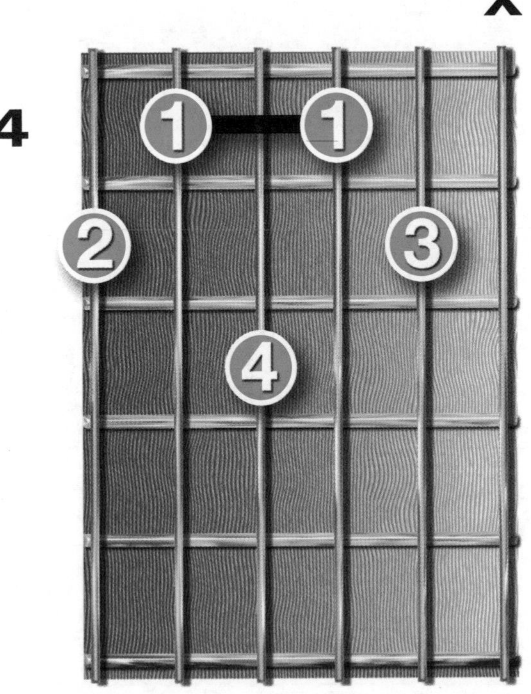

Chord Spelling

1st (A), 3rd (C♯), 5th (E), 7th (G♯)
9th (B)

A+

Augmented

(1st position)

X X

2

Chord Spelling

1st (A), 3rd (C♯), ♯5th (E♯)

A
B♭/A♯
B
C
C♯/D♭
D
E♭/D♯
E
F
F♯/G♭
G
A♭/G♯
Other Chords

A°7

Diminished 7th

(1st position)

4

Chord Spelling

1st (A), ♭3rd (C), ♭5th (E♭), 𝄫7th (G♭)

A⁰

Diminished Triad

(1st position)

Chord Spelling

1st (A), ♭3rd (C), ♭5th (E♭)

A
B♭/A#
B
C
C#/D♭
D
E♭/D#
E
F
F#/G♭
G
A♭/G#
Other Chords

B♭

Major

(1st position)

Chord Spelling

1st (B♭), 3rd (D), 5th (F)

B♭

Major

(2nd position)

Chord Spelling

1st (B♭), 3rd (D), 5th (F)

A
B♭/A#
B
C
C#/D♭
D
E♭/D#
E
F
F#/G♭
G
A♭/G#
Other Chords

B♭m

Minor

(1st position)

Chord Spelling

1st (B♭), ♭3rd (D♭), 5th (F)

B♭m

Minor

(2nd position)

Chord Spelling

1st (B♭), ♭3rd (D♭), 5th (F)

A
B♭/A♯
B
C
C♯/D♭
D
E♭/D♯
E
F
F♯/G♭
G
A♭/G♯
Other Chords

B♭maj7

Major 7th

(1st position)

Chord Spelling

1st (B♭), 3rd (D), 5th (F), 7th (A)

B♭maj7

Major 7th

(2nd position)

Chord Spelling

1st (B♭), 3rd (D), 5th (F), 7th (A)

B♭m7

Minor 7th

(1st position)

Chord Spelling

1st (B♭), ♭3rd (D♭), 5th (F), ♭7th (A♭)

B♭m7

Minor 7th

(2nd position)

Chord Spelling

1st (B♭), ♭3rd (D♭), 5th (F), ♭7th (A♭)

B♭sus4

Suspended 4th

(1st position)

Chord Spelling

1st (B♭), 4th (E♭), 5th (F)

B♭sus4

Suspended 4th

(2nd position)

Chord Spelling

1st (B♭), 4th (E♭), 5th (F)

A
B♭/A♯
B
C
C♯/D♭
D
E♭/D♯
E
F
F♯/G♭
G
A♭/G♯
Other Chords

B♭7sus4

Dominant 7th Suspended 4th

(1st position)

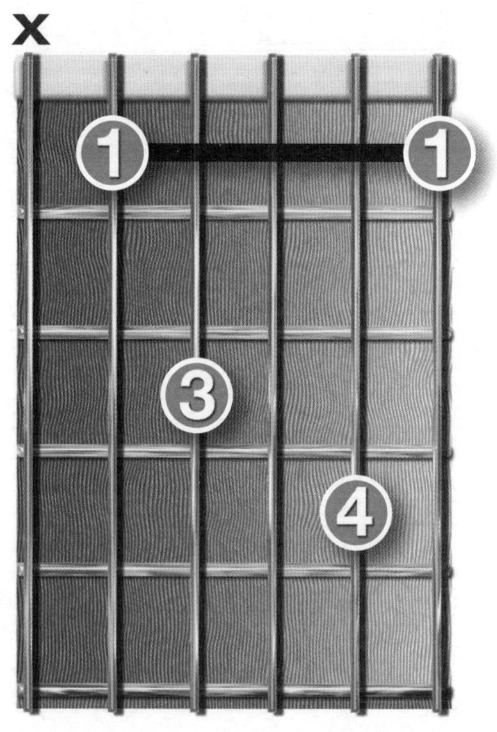

Chord Spelling

1st (B♭), 4th (E♭), 5th (F), ♭7th (A♭)

B♭7sus4

Dominant 7th Suspended 4th

(2nd position)

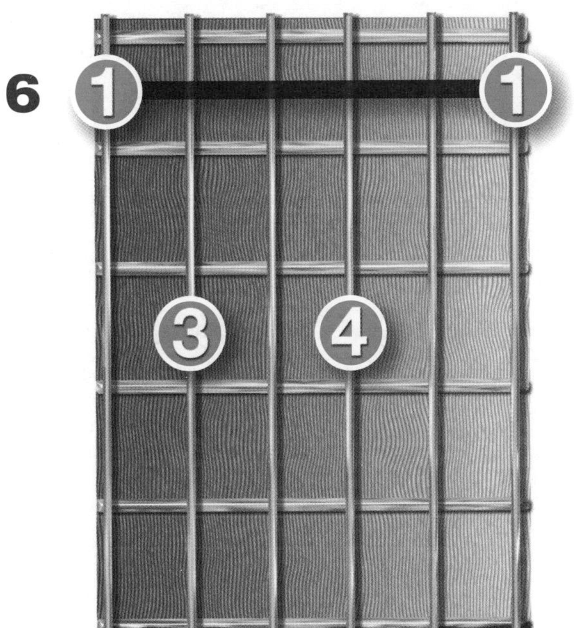

Chord Spelling

1st (B♭), 4th (E♭), 5th (F), ♭7th (A♭)

A
B♭/A♯
B
C
C♯/D♭
D
E♭/D♯
E
F
F♯/G♭
G
A♭/G♯
Other Chords

B♭6

Major 6th

(1st position)

Chord Spelling

1st (B♭), 3rd (D), 5th (F), 6th (G)

B♭6

Major 6th

(2nd position)

5

Chord Spelling

1st (B♭), 3rd (D), 5th (F), 6th (G)

A
B♭/A♯
B
C
C♯/D♭
D
E♭/D♯
E
F
F♯/G♭
G
A♭/G♯
Other Chords

A
B♭/A♯
B
C
C♯/D♭
D
E♭/D♯
E
F
F♯/G♭
G
A♭/G♯
Other Chords

B♭m6

Minor 6th

(1st position)

Chord Spelling

1st (B♭), ♭3rd (D♭), 5th (F), 6th (G)

B♭m6

Minor 6th

(2nd position)

Chord Spelling

1st (B♭), ♭3rd (D♭), 5th (F), 6th (G)

A
B♭/A♯
B
C
C♯/D♭
D
E♭/D♯
E
F
F♯/G♭
G
A♭/G♯
Other Chords

B♭7

Dominant 7th

(1st position)

Chord Spelling

1st (B♭), 3rd (D), 5th (F), ♭7th (A♭)

B♭7

Dominant 7th

(2nd position)

Chord Spelling

1st (B♭), 3rd (D), 5th (F), ♭7th (A♭)

A
B♭/A♯
B
C
C♯/D♭
D
E♭/D♯
E
F
F♯/G♭
G
A♭/G♯
Other Chords

B♭9

Dominant 9th

(1st position)

Chord Spelling

1st (B♭), 3rd (D), 5th (F), ♭7th (A♭), 9th (C)

B♭9

Dominant 9th

(2nd position)

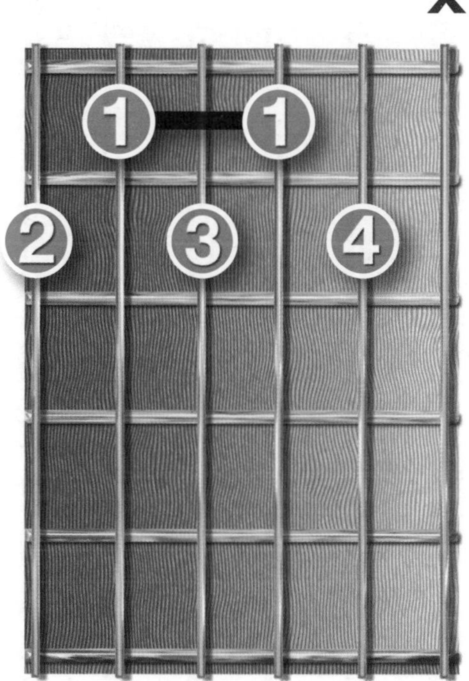

Chord Spelling

1st (B♭), 3rd (D), 5th (F), ♭7th (A♭), 9th (C)

B♭5

5th 'Power Chord'

(1st position)

Chord Spelling

1st (B♭), 5th (F)

B♭6add9

Major 6th add 9th

(1st position)

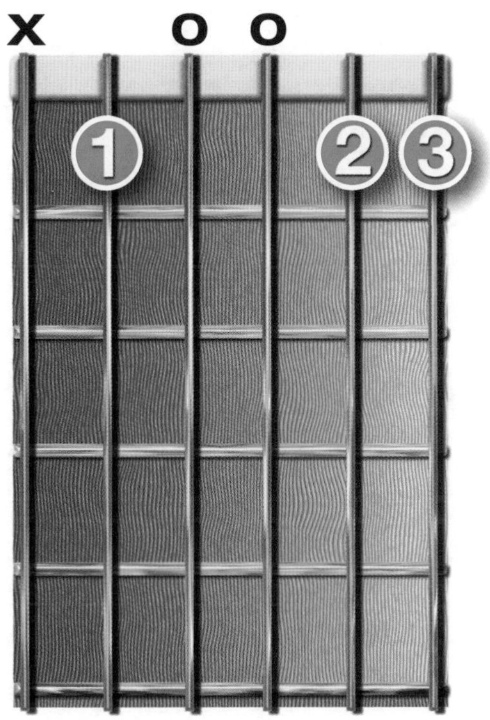

Chord Spelling

1st (B♭), 3rd (D), 5th (F), 6th (G), 9th (C)

A
B♭/A♯
B
C
C♯/D♭
D
E♭/D♯
E
F
F♯/G♭
G
A♭/G♯
Other Chords

B♭11

Dominant 11th

(1st position)

4

Chord Spelling

1st (B♭), 3rd (D), 5th (F), ♭7th (A♭), 9th (C), 11th (E♭)

B♭13

Dominant 13th

(1st position)

6

Chord Spelling

1st (B♭), 3rd (D), 5th (F), ♭7th (A♭),
9th (C), 11th (E♭), 13th (G)

A
B♭/A#
B
C
C#/D♭
D
E♭/D#
E
F
F#/G♭
G
A♭/G#
Other Chords

B♭add9

Major add 9th

(1st position)

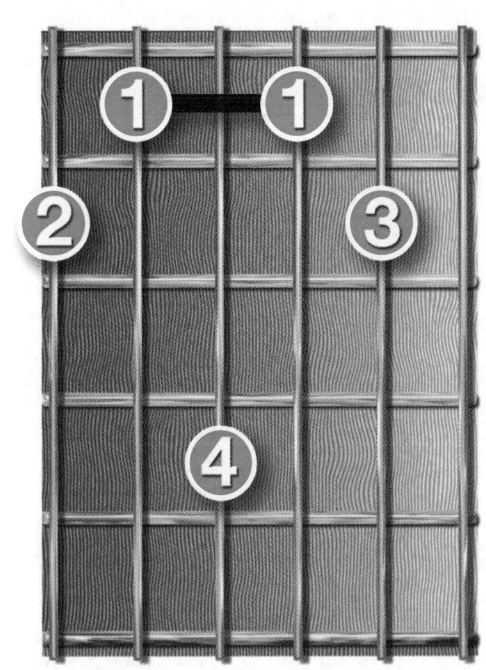

Chord Spelling

1st (B♭), 3rd (D), 5th (F),
9th (C)

B♭m9

Minor 9th

(1st position)

Chord Spelling

1st (B♭), ♭3rd (D♭), 5th (F), ♭7th (A♭), 9th (C)

B♭maj9

Major 9th

(1st position)

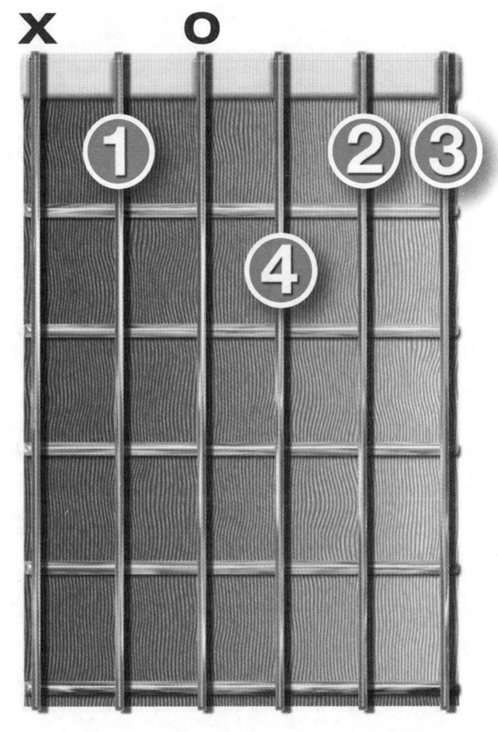

Chord Spelling

1st (B♭), 3rd (D), 5th (F), 7th (A), 9th (C)

B♭+

Augmented

(1st position)

Chord Spelling

1st (B♭), 3rd (D), ♯5th (F♯)

B♭°7

Diminished 7th

(1st position)

Chord Spelling

1st (B♭), ♭3rd (D♭), ♭5th (F♭), 𝄫7th (A𝄫)

B♭°

Diminished Triad

(1st position)

Chord Spelling

1st (B♭), ♭3rd (D♭), ♭5th (F♭)

A
B♭/A♯
B
C
C♯/D♭
D
E♭/D♯
E
F
F♯/G♭
G
A♭/G♯
Other Chords

B

Major

(1st position)

Chord Spelling

1st (B), 3rd (D♯), 5th (F♯)

B

Major

(2nd position)

Chord Spelling

1st (B), 3rd (D♯), 5th (F♯)

A
B♭/A♯
B
C
C♯/D♭
D
E♭/D♯
E
F
F♯/G♭
G
A♭/G♯
Other Chords

A
B♭/A♯
B
C
C♯/D♭
D
E♭/D♯
E
F
F♯/G♭
G
A♭/G♯
Other Chords

Bm

Minor

(1st position)

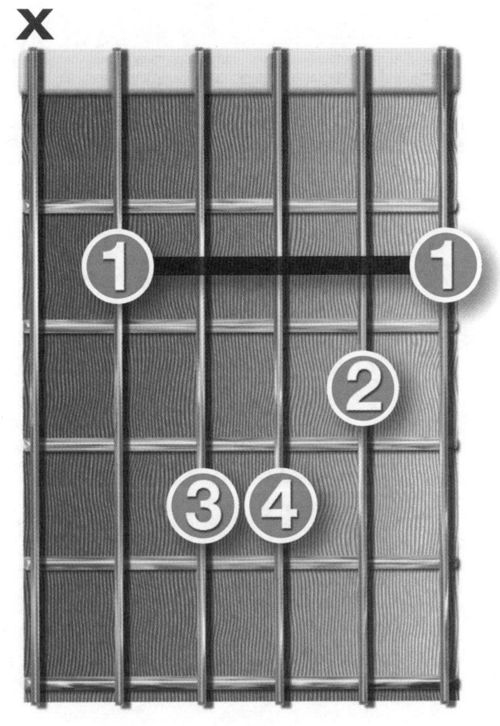

Chord Spelling

1st (B), ♭3rd (D), 5th (F♯)

Bm

Minor

(2nd position)

Chord Spelling

1st (B), ♭3rd (D), 5th (F♯)

Bmaj7

Major 7th

(1st position)

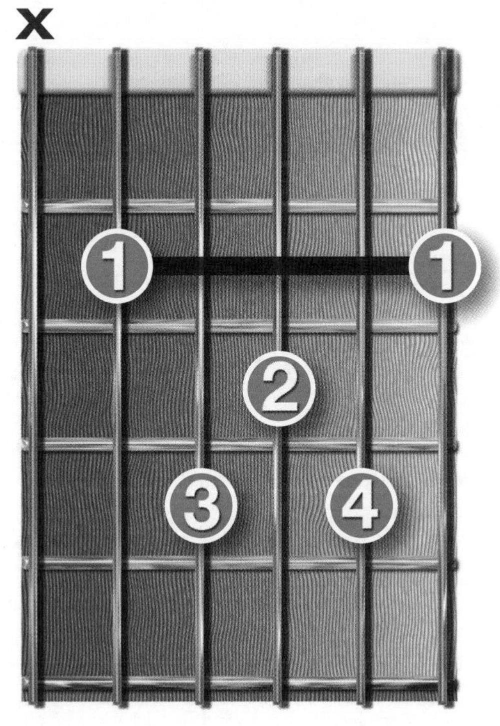

Chord Spelling

1st (B), 3rd (D♯), 5th (F♯), 7th (A♯)

Bmaj7

Major 7th

(2nd position)

6

Chord Spelling

1st (B), 3rd (D♯), 5th (F♯), 7th (A♯)

Bm7

Minor 7th

(1st position)

Chord Spelling

1st (B), ♭3rd (D), 5th (F♯), 7th (A)

Bm7

Minor 7th

(2nd position)

Chord Spelling

1st (B), ♭3rd (D), 5th (F♯), 7th (A)

A
B♭/A♯
B
C
C♯/D♭
D
E♭/D♯
E
F
F♯/G♭
G
A♭/G♯
Other Chords

Bsus4

Suspended 4th

(1st position)

2

Chord Spelling

1st (B), 4th (E), 5th (F♯)

Bsus4

Suspended 4th

(2nd position)

Chord Spelling

1st (B), 4th (E), 5th (F♯)

A
B♭/A♯
B
C
C♯/D♭
D
E♭/D♯
E
F
F♯/G♭
G
A♭/G♯
Other Chords

B7sus4

Dominant 7th Suspended 4th

(1st position)

Chord Spelling

1st (B), 4th (E), 5th (F♯), ♭7th (A)

B7sus4

Dominant 7th Suspended 4th

(2nd position)

2

Chord Spelling

1st (B), 4th (E), 5th (F♯), ♭7th (A)

B6

Major 6th

(1st position)

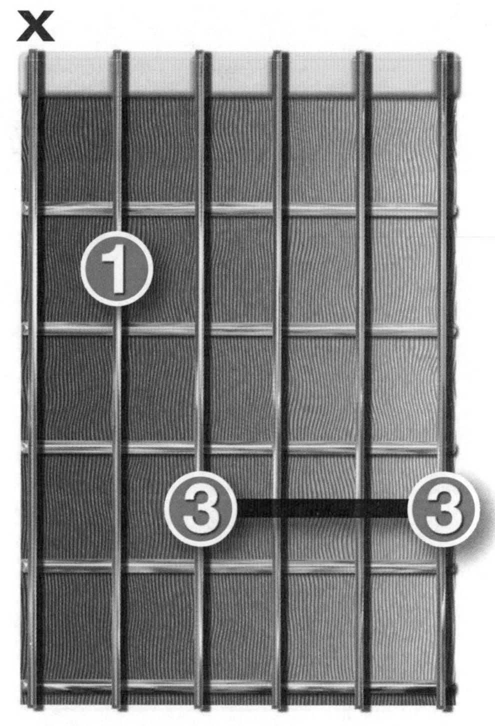

Chord Spelling

1st (B), 3rd (D♯), 5th (F♯), 6th (G♯)

B6

Major 6th

(2nd position)

6

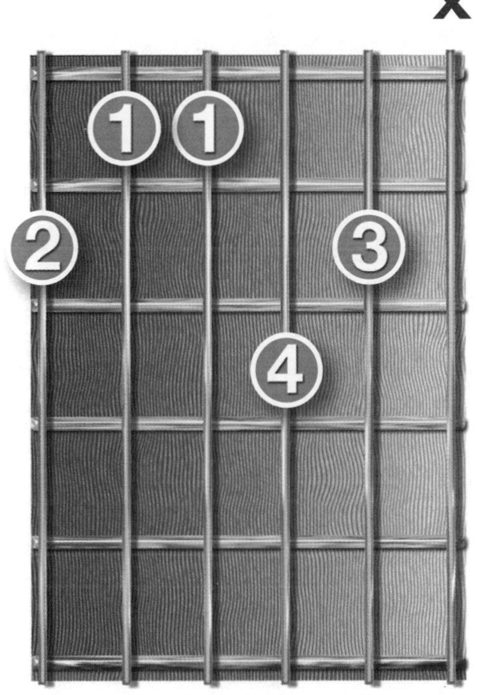

Chord Spelling

1st (B), 3rd (D♯), 5th (F♯), 6th (G♯)

A
B♭/A♯
B
C
C♯/D♭
D
E♭/D♯
E
F
F♯/G♭
G
A♭/G♯
Other Chords

Bm6

Minor 6th

(1st position)

Chord Spelling

1st (B), ♭3rd (D), 5th (F♯), 6th (G♯)

Bm6

Minor 6th

(2nd position)

2

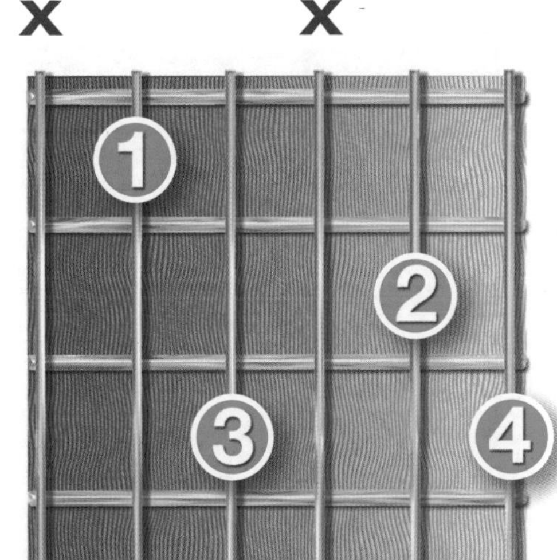

Chord Spelling

1st (B), ♭3rd (D), 5th (F♯), 6th (G♯)

A
B♭/A♯
B
C
C♯/D♭
D
E♭/D♯
E
F
F♯/G♭
G
A♭/G♯
Other Chords

B7

Dominant 7th

(1st position)

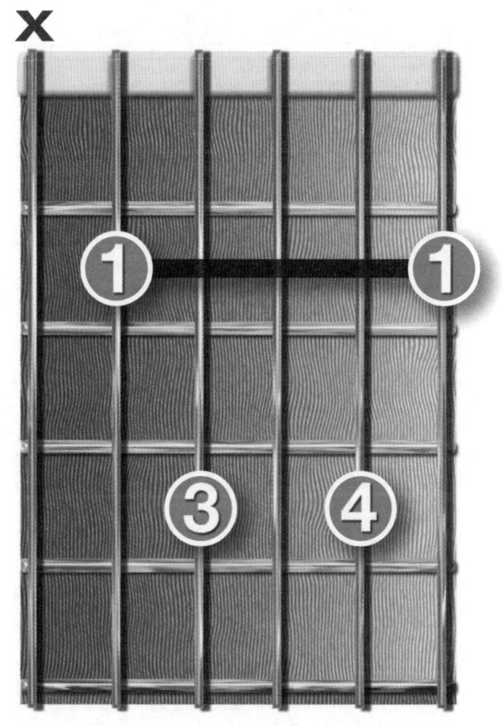

Chord Spelling

1st (B), 3rd (D♯), 5th (F♯), ♭7th (A)

B7

Dominant 7th

(2nd position)

Chord Spelling

1st (B), 3rd (D♯), 5th (F♯), ♭7th (A)

A
B♭/A♯
B
C
C♯/D♭
D
E♭/D♯
E
F
F♯/G♭
G
A♭/G♯
Other Chords

B9

Dominant 9th

(1st position)

Chord Spelling

1st (B), 3rd (D♯), 5th (F♯), ♭7th (A), 9th (C♯)

B9

Dominant 9th

(2nd position)

Chord Spelling

1st (B), 3rd (D♯), 5th (F♯), ♭7th (A), 9th (C♯)

A
B♭/A♯
B
C
C♯/D♭
D
E♭/D♯
E
F
F♯/G♭
G
A♭/G♯
Other Chords

B5

5th 'Power Chord'

(1st position)

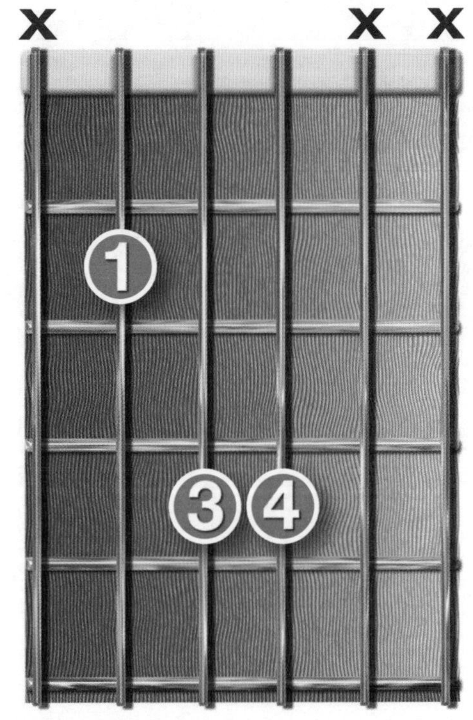

Chord Spelling

1st (B), 5th (F♯)

B6add9

Major 6th add 9th

(1st position)

Chord Spelling

1st (B), 3rd (D♯), 5th (F♯), 6th (G♯), 9th (C♯)

A
B♭/A♯
B
C
C♯/D♭
D
E♭/D♯
E
F
F♯/G♭
G
A♭/G♯
Other Chords

B11

Dominant 11th

(1st position)

Chord Spelling

1st (B), 3rd (D♯), 5th (F♯), ♭7th (A), 9th (C♯), 11th (E)

B13

Dominant 13th

(1st position)

Chord Spelling

1st (B), 3rd (D♯), 5th (F♯), ♭7th (A),
9th (C♯), 11th (E),13th (G♯)

Badd9

Major add 9th

(1st position)

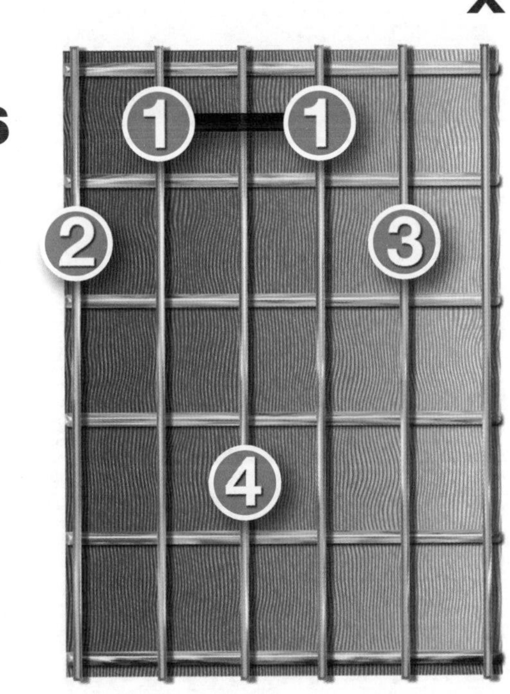

Chord Spelling

1st (B), 3rd (D♯), 5th (F♯),
9th (C♯)

Bm9

Minor 9th

(1st position)

Chord Spelling

1st (B), ♭3rd (D), 5th (F♯), ♭7th (A), 9th (C♯)

Bmaj9

Major 9th

(1st position)

Chord Spelling

1st (B), 3rd (D♯), 5th (F♯), 7th (A♯), 9th (C♯)

B+

Augmented

(1st position)

x x

4

Chord Spelling

1st (B), 3rd (D♯), ♯5th (Fx)

A
B♭/A♯
B
C
C♯/D♭
D
E♭/D♯
E
F
F♯/G♭
G
A♭/G♯
Other Chords

B°7

Diminished 7th

(1st position)

Chord Spelling

1st (B), ♭3rd (D), ♭5th (F), 𝄫7th (A♭)

B°

Diminished Triad

(1st position)

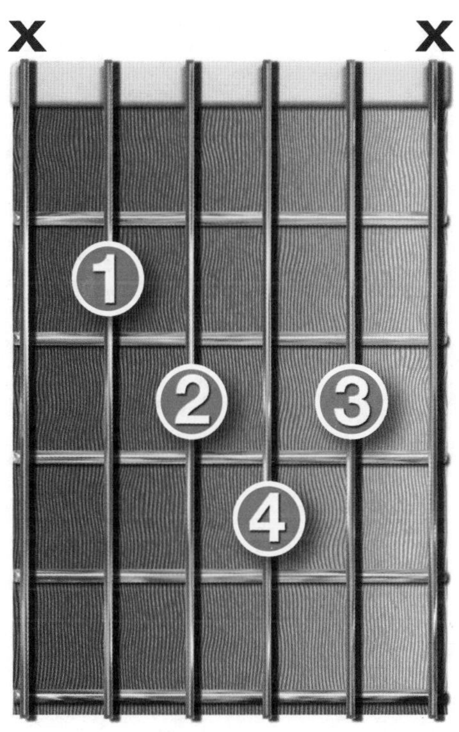

Chord Spelling

1st (B), ♭3rd (D), ♭5th (F)

A
B♭/A♯
B
C
C♯/D♭
D
E♭/D♯
E
F
F♯/G♭
G
A♭/G♯
Other Chords

C

Major

(1st position)

Chord Spelling

1st (C), 3rd (E), 5th (G)

C

Major

(2nd position)

3

Chord Spelling

1st (C), 3rd (E), 5th (G)

A
B♭/A♯
B
C
C♯/D♭
D
E♭/D♯
E
F
F♯/G♭
G
A♭/G♯
Other Chords

Cm

Minor

(1st position)

3

Chord Spelling

1st (C), ♭3rd (E♭), 5th (G)

Cm

Minor

(2nd position)

Chord Spelling

1st (C), ♭3rd (E♭), 5th (G)

A
B♭/A♯
B
C
C♯/D♭
D
E♭/D♯
E
F
F♯/G♭
G
A♭/G♯
Other Chords

Cmaj7

Major 7th

(1st position)

Chord Spelling

1st (C), 3rd (E), 5th (G), 7th (B)

Cmaj7

Major 7th

(2nd position)

3

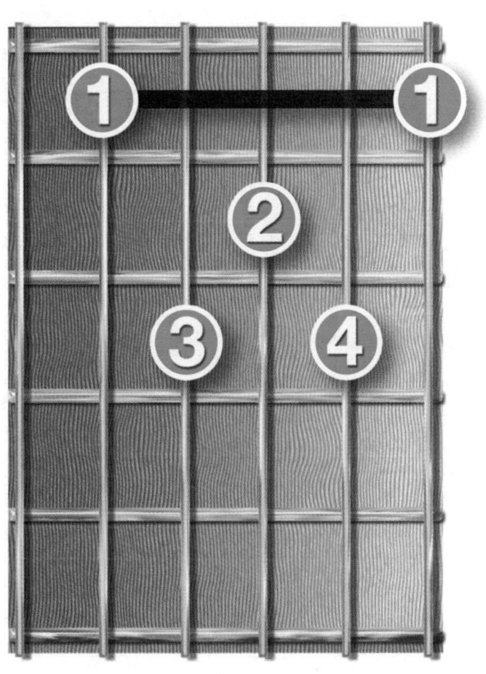

Chord Spelling

1st (C), 3rd (E), 5th (G), 7th (B)

A
B♭/A♯
B
C
C♯/D♭
D
E♭/D♯
E
F
F♯/G♭
G
A♭/G♯
Other Chords

Cm7

Minor 7th

(1st position)

Chord Spelling

1st (C), ♭3rd (E♭), 5th (G), ♭7th (B♭)

Cm7

Minor 7th

(2nd position)

8

Chord Spelling

1st (C), ♭3rd (E♭), 5th (G), ♭7th (B♭)

Csus4

Suspended 4th

(1st position)

Chord Spelling

1st (C), 4th (F), 5th (G)

Csus4

Suspended 4th

(2nd position)

3

Chord Spelling

1st (C), 4th (F), 5th (G)

A
B♭/A♯
B
C
C♯/D♭
D
E♭/D♯
E
F
F♯/G♭
G
A♭/G♯
Other Chords

C7sus4

Dominant 7th Suspended 4th

(1st position)

Chord Spelling

1st (C), 4th (F), 5th (G), ♭7th (B♭)

C7sus4

Dominant 7th Suspended 4th

(2nd position)

3

Chord Spelling

1st (C), 4th (F), 5th (G), ♭7th (B♭)

C6

Major 6th

(1st position)

Chord Spelling

1st (C), 3rd (E), 5th (G), 6th (A)

C6

Major 6th

(2nd position)

o

7

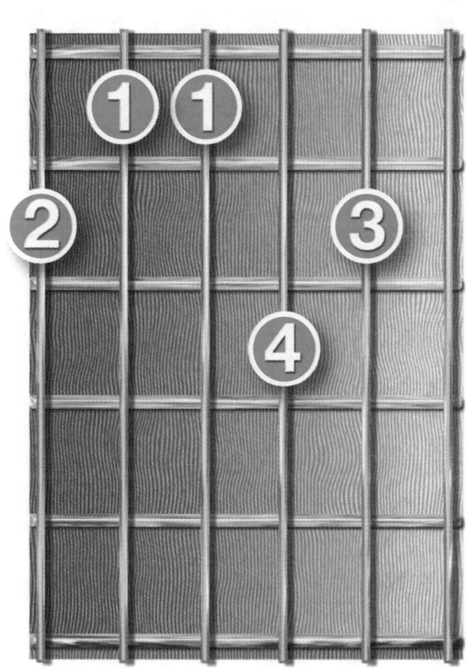

Chord Spelling

1st (C), 3rd (E), 5th (G), 6th (A)

A
B♭/A♯
B
C
C♯/D♭
D
E♭/D♯
E
F
F♯/G♭
G
A♭/G♯
Other Chords

Cm6

Minor 6th

(1st position)

Chord Spelling

1st (C), ♭3rd (E♭), 5th (G), 6th (A)

Cm6

Minor 6th

(2nd position)

Chord Spelling

1st (C), ♭3rd (E♭), 5th (G), 6th (A)

A
B♭/A♯
B
C
C♯/D♭
D
E♭/D♯
E
F
F♯/G♭
G
A♭/G♯
Other Chords

C7

Dominant 7th

(1st position)

Chord Spelling

1st (C), 3rd (E), 5th (G), ♭7th (B♭)

C7

Dominant 7th

(2nd position)

3

Chord Spelling

1st (C), 3rd (E), 5th (G), ♭7th (B♭)

A
B♭/A♯
B
C
C♯/D♭
D
E♭/D♯
E
F
F♯/G♭
G
A♭/G♯
Other Chords

C9

Dominant 9th

(1st position)

Chord Spelling

1st (C), 3rd (E), 5th (G), ♭7th (B♭), 9th (D)

C9

Dominant 9th

(2nd position)

o

7

Chord Spelling

1st (C), 3rd (E), 5th (G), ♭7th (B♭), 9th (D)

A
B♭/A♯
B
C
C♯/D♭
D
E♭/D♯
E
F
F♯/G♭
G
A♭/G♯
Other Chords

A
B♭/A♯
B
C
C♯/D♭
D
E♭/D♯
E
F
F♯/G♭
G
A♭/G♯
Other Chords

C5

5th 'Power Chord'

(1st position)

3

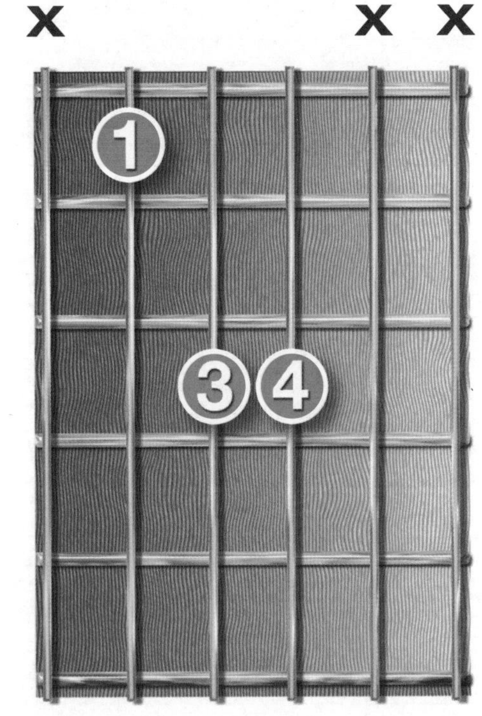

Chord Spelling

1st (C), 5th (G)

C6add9

Major 6th add 9th

(1st position)

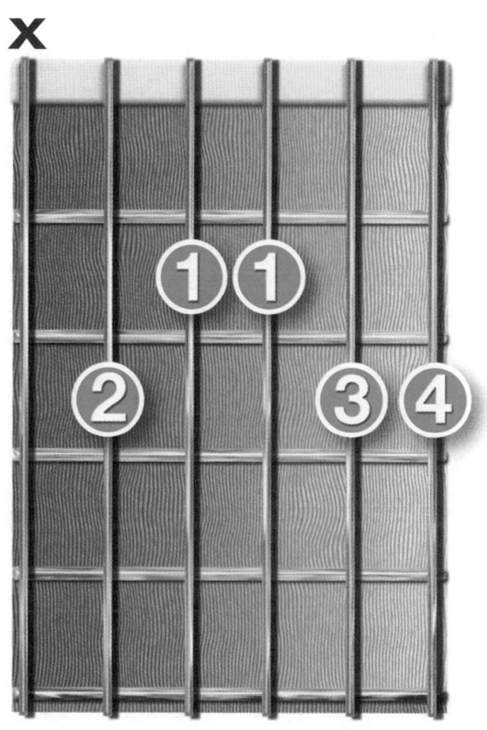

Chord Spelling

1st (C), 3rd (E), 5th (G), 6th (A), 9th (D)

A
B♭/A♯
B
C
C♯/D♭
D
E♭/D♯
E
F
F♯/G♭
G
A♭/G♯
Other Chords

C11

Dominant 11th

(1st position)

Chord Spelling

1st (C), 3rd (E), 5th (G), ♭7th (B♭),
9th (D), 11th (F)

C13

Dominant 13th

(1st position)

x

2

Chord Spelling

1st (C), 3rd (E), 5th (G), ♭7th (B♭),
9th (D), 11th (D), 13th (A)

A
B♭/A♯
B
C
C♯/D♭
D
E♭/D♯
E
F
F♯/G♭
G
A♭/G♯
Other Chords

Cadd9

Major add 9th

(1st position)

Chord Spelling

1st (C), 3rd (E), 5th (G), 9th (D)

Cm9

Minor 9th

(1st position)

6

Chord Spelling

1st (C), ♭3rd (E♭), 5th (G), ♭7th (B♭),
9th (D)

A
B♭/A♯
B
C
C♯/D♭
D
E♭/D♯
E
F
F♯/G♭
G
A♭/G♯
Other Chords

Cmaj9

Major 9th

(1st position)

Chord Spelling

1st (C), 3rd (E), 5th (G), 7th (B),
9th (D)

C+

Augmented

(1st position)

Chord Spelling

1st (C), 3rd (E), ♯5th (G♯)

A
B♭/A♯
B
C
C♯/D♭
D
E♭/D♯
E
F
F♯/G♭
G
A♭/G♯
Other Chords

A
B♭/A♯
B
C
C♯/D♭
D
E♭/D♯
E
F
F♯/G♭
G
A♭/G♯
Other Chords

C^{o}7

Diminished 7th

(1st position)

Chord Spelling

1st (C), ♭3rd (E♭), ♭5th (G♭), 𝄫7th (B𝄫)

C⁰

Diminished Triad

(1st position)

Chord Spelling

1st (C), ♭3rd (E♭), ♭5th (G♭)

C♯

Major

(1st position)

Chord Spelling

1st (C♯), 3rd (E♯), 5th (G♯)

C♯

Major

(2nd position)

4

Chord Spelling

1st (C♯), 3rd (E♯), 5th (G♯)

A
B♭/A♯
B
C
C♯/D♭
D
E♭/D♯
E
F
F♯/G♭
G
A♭/G♯
Other Chords

C♯m

Minor

(1st position)

Chord Spelling

1st (C♯), ♭3rd (E), 5th (G♯)

C♯m

Minor

(2nd position)

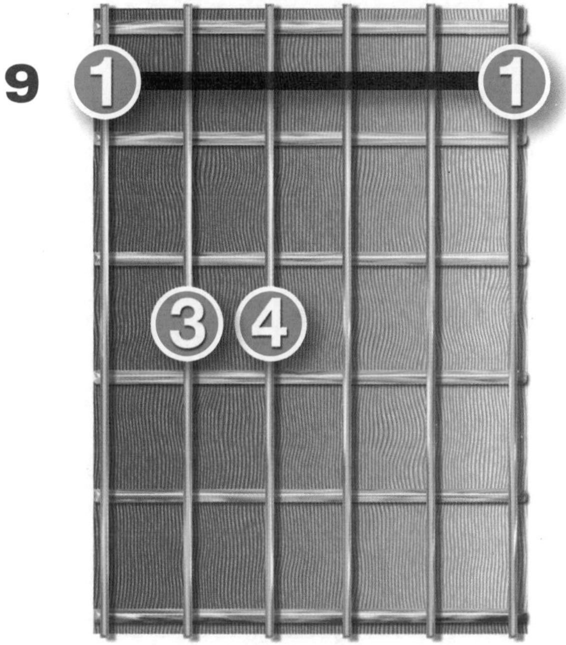

9

Chord Spelling

1st (C♯), ♭3rd (E), 5th (G♯)

C♯maj7

Major 7th

(1st position)

Chord Spelling

1st (C♯), 3rd (E♯), 5th (G♯), 7th (B♯)

C♯maj7

Major 7th

(2nd position)

4

Chord Spelling

1st (C♯), 3rd (E♯), 5th (G♯), 7th (B♯)

A
B♭/A♯
B
C
C♯/D♭
D
E♭/D♯
E
F
F♯/G♭
G
A♭/G♯
Other Chords

C♯m7

Minor 7th

(1st position)

2

Chord Spelling

1st (C♯), ♭3rd (E), 5th (G♯), ♭7th (B)

C♯m7

Minor 7th

(2nd position)

4

Chord Spelling

1st (C♯), ♭3rd (E), 5th (G♯), ♭7th (B)

C♯sus4

Suspended 4th

(1st position)

4

Chord Spelling

1st (C♯), 4th (F♯), 5th (G♯)

C♯sus4

Suspended 4th

(2nd position)

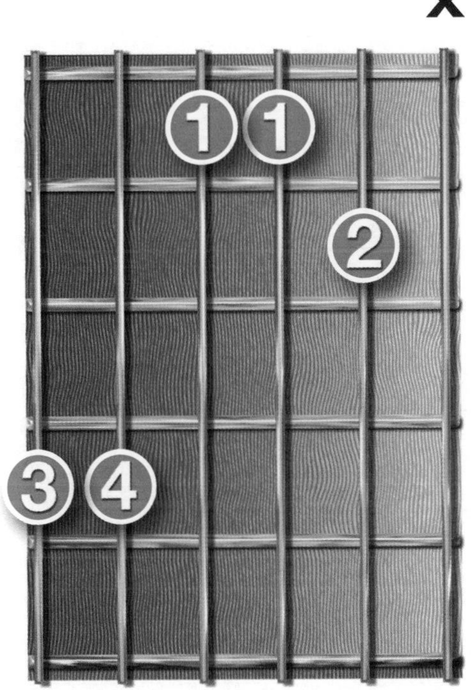

Chord Spelling

1st (C♯), 4th (F♯), 5th (G♯)

A
B♭/A♯
B
C
C♯/D♭
D
E♭/D♯
E
F
F♯/G♭
G
A♭/G♯
Other Chords

C♯7sus4

Dominant 7th Suspended 4th

(1st position)

4

Chord Spelling

1st (C♯), 4th (F♯), 5th (G♯), ♭7th (B)

C♯7sus4

Dominant 7th Suspended 4th

(2nd position)

4

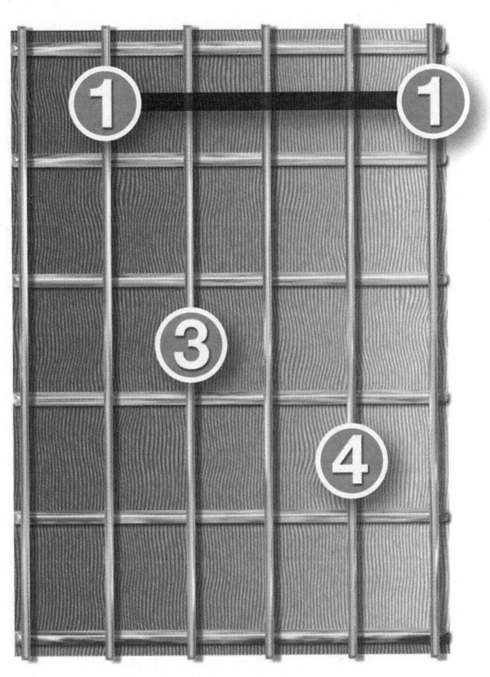

Chord Spelling

1st (C♯), 4th (F♯), 5th (G♯), ♭7th (B)

A
B♭/A♯
B
C
C♯/D♭
D
E♭/D♯
E
F
F♯/G♭
G
A♭/G♯
Other Chords

A
B♭/A♯
B
C
C♯/D♭
D
E♭/D♯
E
F
F♯/G♭
G
A♭/G♯
Other Chords

C♯6

Major 6th

(1st position)

4

Chord Spelling

1st (C♯), 3rd (E♯), 5th (G♯), 6th (A♯)

C♯6

Major 6th

(2nd position)

8

Chord Spelling

1st (C♯), 3rd (E♯), 5th (G♯), 6th (A♯)

C♯m6

Minor 6th

(1st position)

Chord Spelling

1st (C♯), ♭3rd (E), 5th (G♯), 6th (A♯)

C♯m6

Minor 6th

(2nd position)

4

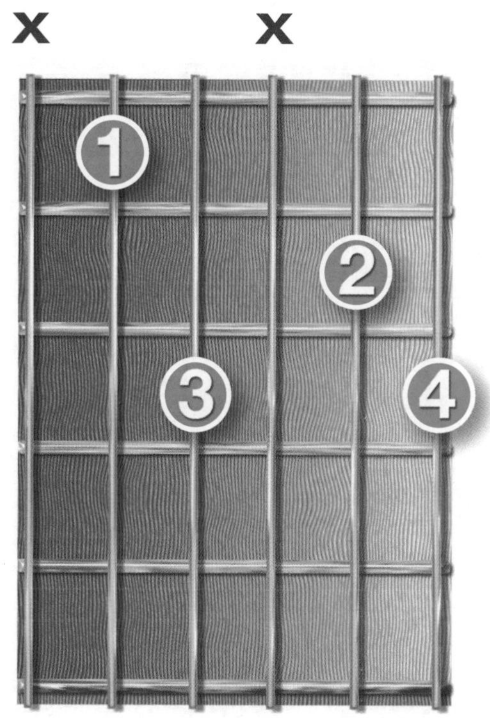

Chord Spelling

1st (C♯), ♭3rd (E), 5th (G♯), 6th (A♯)

A
B♭/A♯
B
C
C♯/D♭
D
E♭/D♯
E
F
F♯/G♭
G
A♭/G♯
Other Chords

A
B♭/A♯
B
C
C♯/D♭
D
E♭/D♯
E
F
F♯/G♭
G
A♭/G♯
Other Chords

C♯7

Dominant 7th

(1st position)

Chord Spelling

1st (C♯), 3rd (E♯), 5th (G♯), ♭7th (B)

C♯7

Dominant 7th

(2nd position)

4

Chord Spelling

1st (C♯), 3rd (E♯), 5th (G♯), ♭7th (B)

C♯9

Dominant 9th

(1st position)

3

Chord Spelling

1st (C♯), 3rd (E♯), 5th (G♯), ♭7th (B), 9th (D♯)

C♯9

Dominant 9th

(2nd position)

8

Chord Spelling

1st (C♯), 3rd (E♯), 5th (G♯), ♭7th (B), 9th (D♯)

A
B♭/A♯
B
C
C♯/D♭
D
E♭/D♯
E
F
F♯/G♭
G
A♭/G♯
Other Chords

C♯5

5th 'Power Chord'

(1st position)

Chord Spelling

1st (C♯), 5th (G♯)

C♯6add9

Major 6th add 9th

(1st position)

Chord Spelling

1st (C♯), 3rd (E♯), 5th (G♯), 6th (A♯), 9th (D♯)

A
B♭/A♯
B
C
C♯/D♭
D
E♭/D♯
E
F
F♯/G♭
G
A♭/G♯
Other Chords

C♯11

Dominant 11th

(1st position)

2

Chord Spelling

1st (C♯), 3rd (E♯), 5th (G♯), ♭7th (B), 9th (D♯), 11th (F♯)

C♯13

Dominant 13th

(1st position)

3

Chord Spelling

1st (C♯), 3rd (E♯), 5th (G♯), ♭7th (B),
9th (D♯), 11th (F♯), 13th (A♯)

C♯add9

Major add 9th

(1st position)

Chord Spelling

1st (C♯), 3rd (E♯), 5th (G♯),
9th (D♯)

C♯m9

Minor 9th

(1st position)

7

Chord Spelling

1st (C♯), ♭3rd (E), 5th (G♯), ♭7th (B), 9th (D♯)

A
B♭/A♯
B
C
C♯/D♭
D
E♭/D♯
E
F
F♯/G♭
G
A♭/G♯
Other Chords

C♯maj9

Major 9th

(1st position)

3

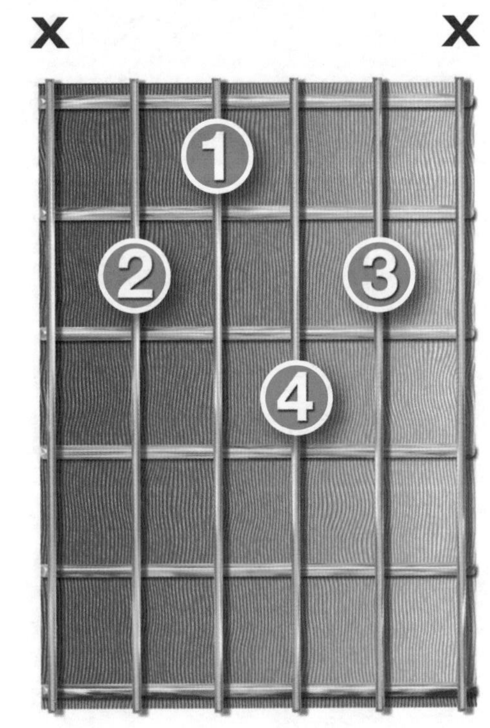

Chord Spelling

1st (C♯), 3rd (E♯), 5th (G♯), 7th (B♯), 9th (D♯)

C♯+

Augmented

(1st position)

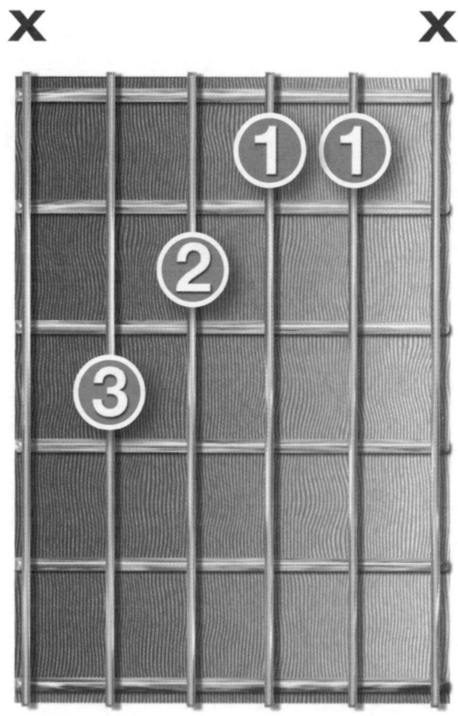

Chord Spelling

1st (C♯), 3rd (E♯), ♯5th (Gx)

C♯°7

Diminished 7th

(1st position)

Chord Spelling

1st (C♯), ♭3rd (E), ♭5th (G), 𝄫7th (B♭)

C♯°

Diminished Triad

(1st position)

Chord Spelling

1st (C♯), ♭3rd (E), ♭5th (G)

A
B♭/A♯
B
C
C♯/D♭
D
E♭/D♯
E
F
F♯/G♭
G
A♭/G♯
Other Chords

D

Major

(1st position)

Chord Spelling

1st (D), 3rd (F♯), 5th (A)

A
B♭/A♯
B
C
C♯/D♭
D
E♭/D♯
E
F
F♯/G♭
G
A♭/G♯
Other Chords

D

Major

(2nd position)

X

5

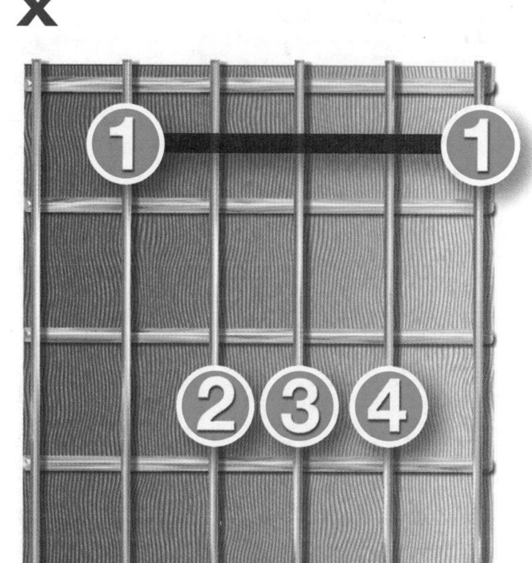

Chord Spelling

1st (D), 3rd (F♯), 5th (A)

A
B♭/A♯
B
C
C♯/D♭
D
E♭/D♯
E
F
F♯/G♭
G
A♭/G♯
Other Chords

Dm

Minor

(1st position)

Chord Spelling

1st (D), ♭3rd (F), 5th (A)

Dm

Minor

(2nd position)

5

Chord Spelling

1st (D), ♭3rd (F), 5th (A)

A
B♭/A♯
B
C
C♯/D♭
D
E♭/D♯
E
F
F♯/G♭
G
A♭/G♯
Other Chords

Dmaj7

Major 7th

(1st position)

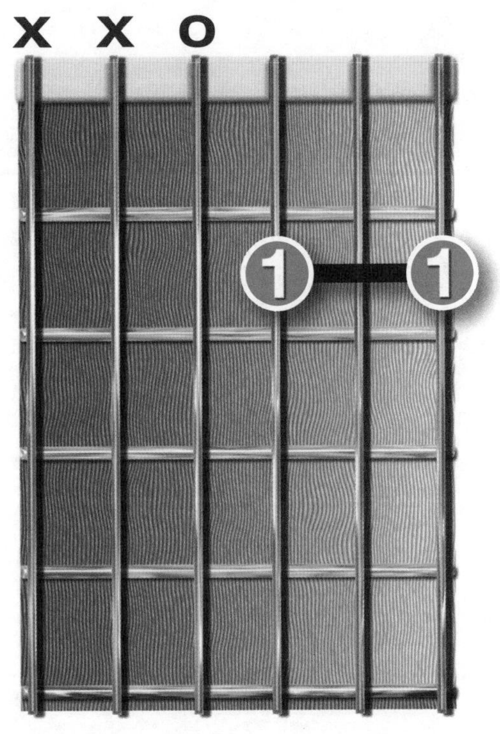

Chord Spelling

1st (D), 3rd (F♯), 5th (A), 7th (C♯)

Dmaj7

Major 7th

(2nd position)

Chord Spelling

1st (D), 3rd (F♯), 5th (A), 7th (C♯)

A
B♭/A♯
B
C
C♯/D♭
D
E♭/D♯
E
F
F♯/G♭
G
A♭/G♯
Other Chords

A
B♭/A♯
B
C
C♯/D♭
D
E♭/D♯
E
F
F♯/G♭
G
A♭/G♯
Other Chords

Dm7

Minor 7th

(1st position)

Chord Spelling

1st (D), ♭3rd (F), 5th (A), ♭7th (C)

Dm7

Minor 7th

(2nd position)

5

Chord Spelling

1st (D), ♭3rd (F), 5th (A), ♭7th (C)

Dsus4

Suspended 4th

(1st position)

Chord Spelling

1st (D), 4th (G), 5th (A)

Dsus4

Suspended 4th

(2nd position)

5

Chord Spelling

1st (D), 4th (G), 5th (A)

A
B♭/A♯
B
C
C♯/D♭
D
E♭/D♯
E
F
F♯/G♭
G
A♭/G♯
Other Chords

D7sus4

Dominant 7th Suspended 4th

(1st position)

Chord Spelling

1st (D), 4th (G), 5th (A), ♭7th (C)

D7sus4

Dominant 7th Suspended 4th

(2nd position)

Chord Spelling

1st (D), 4th (G), 5th (A), ♭7th (C)

A
B♭/A♯
B
C
C♯/D♭
D
E♭/D♯
E
F
F♯/G♭
G
A♭/G♯
Other Chords

D6

Major 6th

(1st position)

Chord Spelling

1st (D), 3rd (F♯), 5th (A), 6th (B)

D6

Major 6th

(2nd position)

5

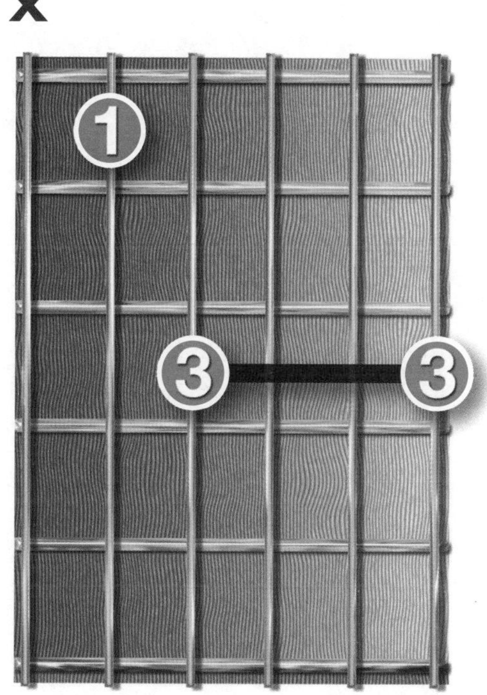

Chord Spelling

1st (D), 3rd (F♯), 5th (A), 6th (B)

A
B♭/A♯
B
C
C♯/D♭
D
E♭/D♯
E
F
F♯/G♭
G
A♭/G♯
Other Chords

Dm6

Minor 6th

(1st position)

Chord Spelling

1st (D), ♭3rd (F), 5th (A), 6th (B)

Dm6

Minor 6th

(2nd position)

Chord Spelling

1st (D), ♭3rd (F), 5th (A), 6th (B)

A
B♭/A♯
B
C
C♯/D♭
D
E♭/D♯
E
F
F♯/G♭
G
A♭/G♯
Other Chords

A
B♭/A♯
B
C
C♯/D♭
D
E♭/D♯
E
F
F♯/G♭
G
A♭/G♯
Other Chords

D7

Dominant 7th

(1st position)

Chord Spelling

1st (D), 3rd (F♯), 5th (A), ♭7th (C)

D7

Dominant 7th

(2nd position)

5

Chord Spelling

1st (D), 3rd (F♯), 5th (A), ♭7th (C)

D9

Dominant 9th

(1st position)

Chord Spelling

1st (D), 3rd (F♯), 5th (A), ♭7th (C), 9th (E)

D9

Dominant 9th

(2nd position)

x

9

Chord Spelling

1st (D), 3rd (F♯), 5th (A), ♭7th (C), 9th (E)

A
B♭/A♯
B
C
C♯/D♭
D
E♭/D♯
E
F
F♯/G♭
G
A♭/G♯
Other Chords

D5

5th 'Power Chord'

(1st position)

Chord Spelling

1st (D), 5th (A)

D6add9

Major 6th add 9th

(1st position)

4

Chord Spelling

1st (D), 3rd (F♯), 5th (A), 6th (B),
9th (E)

A
B♭/A♯
B
C
C♯/D♭
D
E♭/D♯
E
F
F♯/G♭
G
A♭/G♯
Other Chords

D11

Dominant 11th

(1st position)

3

Chord Spelling

1st (D), 3rd (F♯), 5th (A), ♭7th (C),
9th (E), 11th (G)

D13

Dominant 13th

(1st position)

4

Chord Spelling

1st (D), 3rd (F♯), 5th (A), ♭7th (C),
9th (E), 11th (G), 13th (B)

A
B♭/A♯
B
C
C♯/D♭
D
E♭/D♯
E
F
F♯/G♭
G
A♭/G♯
Other Chords

Dadd9

Major add 9th

(1st position)

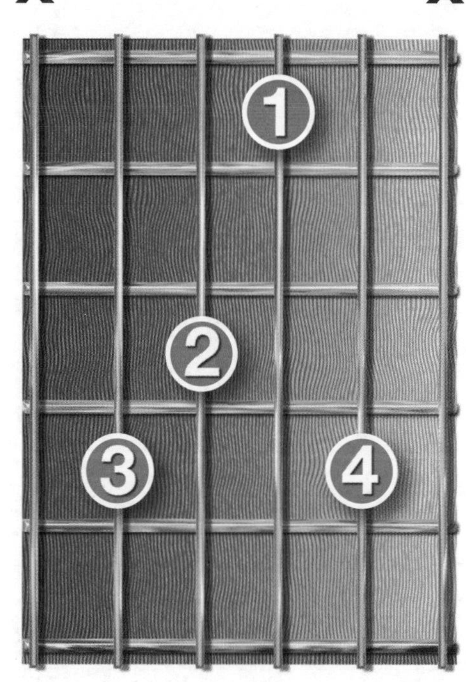

Chord Spelling

1st (D), 3rd (F♯), 5th (A), 9th (E)

Dm9

Minor 9th

(1st position)

Chord Spelling

1st (D), ♭3rd (F), 5th (A), ♭7th (C),
9th (E)

A
B♭/A♯
B
C
C♯/D♭
D
E♭/D♯
E
F
F♯/G♭
G
A♭/G♯
Other Chords

Dmaj9

Major 9th

(1st position)

Chord Spelling

1st (D), 3rd (F♯), 5th (A), 7th (C♯), 9th (E)

D+

Augmented

(1st position)

3

Chord Spelling

1st (D), 3rd (F♯), ♯5th (A♯)

A
B♭/A♯
B
C
C♯/D♭
D
E♭/D♯
E
F
F♯/G♭
G
A♭/G♯
Other Chords

A
B♭/A♯
B
C
C♯/D♭
D
E♭/D♯
E
F
F♯/G♭
G
A♭/G♯
Other Chords

D°7

Diminished 7th

(1st position)

Chord Spelling

1st (D), ♭3rd (F), ♭5th (A♭), 𝄫7th (C♭)

D^0

Diminished Triad

(1st position)

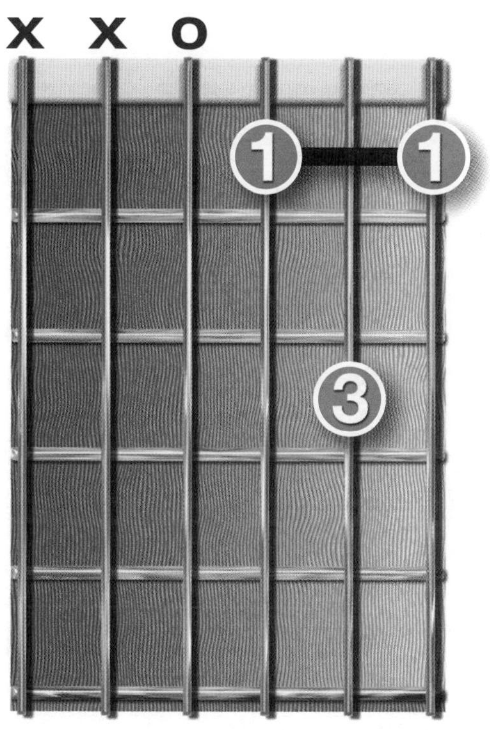

Chord Spelling

1st (D), ♭3rd (F), ♭5th (A♭)

E♭

Major

(1st position)

x

3

Chord Spelling

1st (E♭), 3rd (G), 5th (B♭)

E♭

Major

(2nd position)

6

Chord Spelling

1st (E♭), 3rd (G), 5th (B♭)

A
B♭/A♯
B
C
C♯/D♭
D
E♭/D♯
E
F
F♯/G♭
G
A♭/G♯
Other Chords

E♭m

Minor

(1st position)

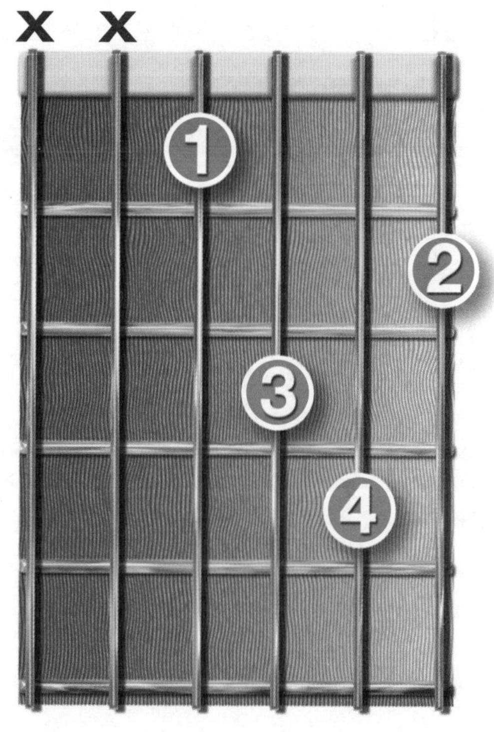

Chord Spelling

1st (E♭), ♭3rd (G♭), 5th (B♭)

E♭m

Minor

(2nd position)

6

Chord Spelling

1st (E♭), ♭3rd (G♭), 5th (B♭)

A
B♭/A♯
B
C
C♯/D♭
D
E♭/D♯
E
F
F♯/G♭
G
A♭/G♯
Other Chords

E♭maj7

Major 7th

(1st position)

3

Chord Spelling

1st (E♭), 3rd (G), 5th (B♭), 7th (D)

E♭maj7

Major 7th

(2nd position)

6

Chord Spelling

1st (E♭), 3rd (G), 5th (B♭), 7th (D)

A
B♭/A♯
B
C
C♯/D♭
D
E♭/D♯
E
F
F♯/G♭
G
A♭/G♯
Other Chords

E♭m7

Minor 7th

(1st position)

4

Chord Spelling

1st (E♭), ♭3rd (G♭), 5th (B♭), ♭7th (D♭)

E♭m7

Minor 7th

(2nd position)

Chord Spelling

1st (E♭), ♭3rd (G♭), 5th (B♭), ♭7th (D♭)

E♭sus4

Suspended 4th

(1st position)

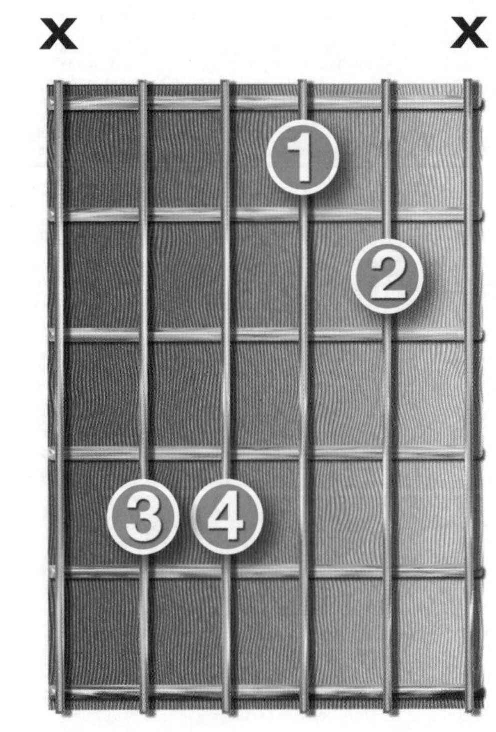

Chord Spelling

1st (E♭), 4th (A♭), 5th (B♭)

E♭sus4

Suspended 4th

(2nd position)

6

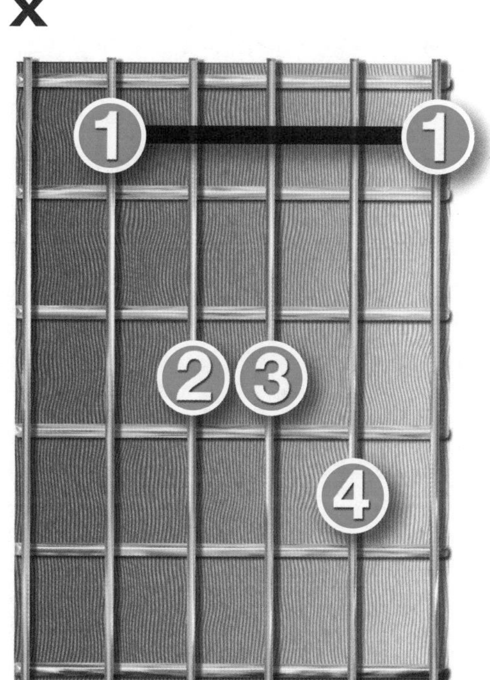

Chord Spelling

1st (E♭), 4th (A♭), 5th (B♭)

A
B♭/A♯
B
C
C♯/D♭
D
E♭/D♯
E
F
F♯/G♭
G
A♭/G♯
Other Chords

E♭7sus4

Dominant 7th Suspended 4th

(1st position)

Chord Spelling

1st (E♭), 4th (A♭), 5th (B♭), ♭7th (D♭)

E♭7sus4

Dominant 7th Suspended 4th

(2nd position)

6

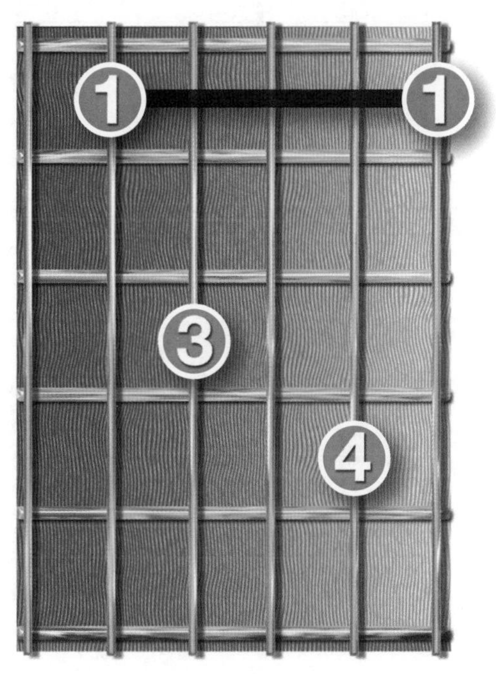

Chord Spelling

1st (E♭), 4th (A♭), 5th (B♭), ♭7th (D♭)

E♭6

Major 6th

(1st position)

Chord Spelling

1st (E♭), 3rd (G), 5th (B♭), 6th (C)

A
B♭/A♯
B
C
C♯/D♭
D
E♭/D♯
E
F
F♯/G♭
G
A♭/G♯
Other Chords

E♭6

Major 6th

(2nd position)

6

Chord Spelling

1st (E♭), 3rd (G), 5th (B♭), 6th (C)

A
B♭/A♯
B
C
C♯/D♭
D
E♭/D♯
E
F
F♯/G♭
G
A♭/G♯
Other Chords

E♭m6

Minor 6th

(1st position)

4

Chord Spelling

1st (E♭), ♭3rd (G♭), 5th (B♭), 6th (C)

E♭m6

Minor 6th

(2nd position)

Chord Spelling

1st (E♭), ♭3rd (G♭), 5th (B♭), 6th (C)

E♭7

Dominant 7th

(1st position)

4

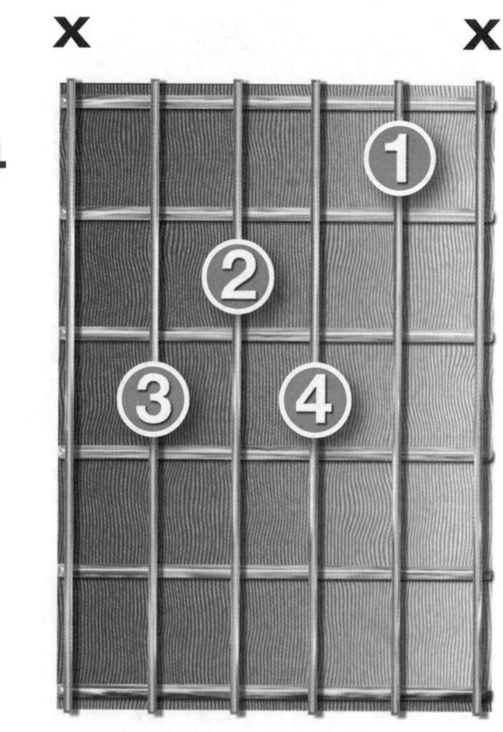

Chord Spelling

1st (E♭), 3rd (G), 5th (B♭), ♭7th (D♭)

E♭7

Dominant 7th

(2nd position)

6

Chord Spelling

1st (E♭), 3rd (G), 5th (B♭), ♭7th (D♭)

E♭9

Dominant 9th

(1st position)

Chord Spelling

1st (E♭), 3rd (G), 5th (B♭), ♭7th (D♭), 9th (F)

E♭9

Dominant 9th

(2nd position)

X

5

Chord Spelling

1st (E♭), 3rd (G), 5th (B♭), ♭7th (D♭), 9th (F)

A
B♭/A♯
B
C
C♯/D♭
D
E♭/D♯
E
F
F♯/G♭
G
A♭/G♯
Other Chords

E♭5

5th 'Power Chord'

(1st position)

6

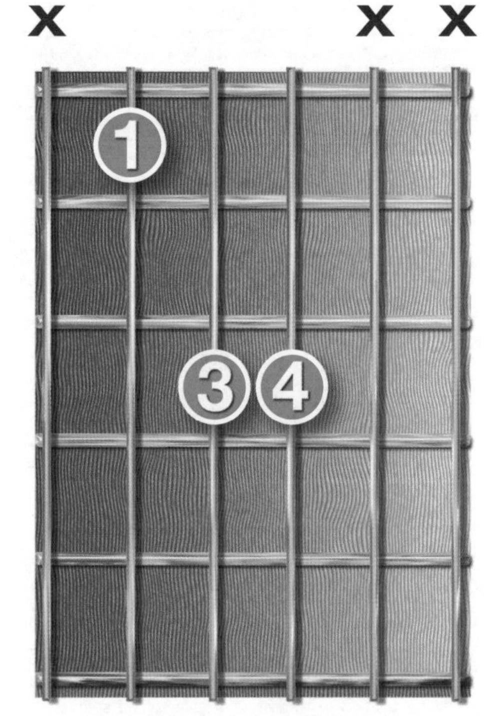

Chord Spelling

1st (E♭), 5th (B♭)

E♭6add9

Major 6th add 9th

(1st position)

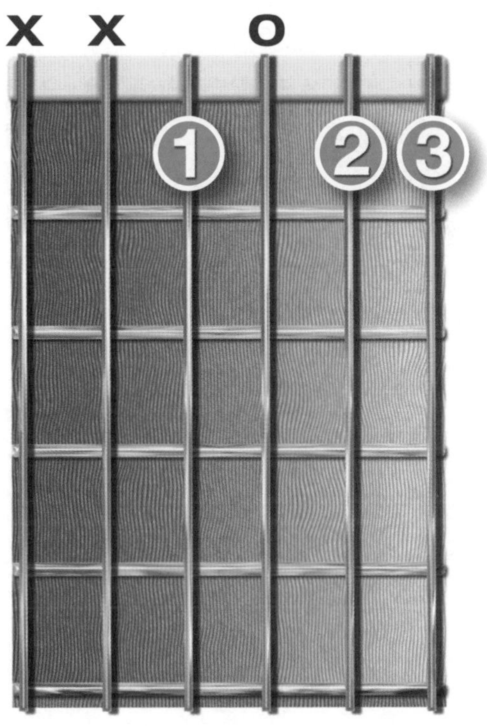

Chord Spelling

1st (E♭), 3rd (G), 5th (B♭), 6th (C), 9th (F)

E♭11

Dominant 11th

(1st position)

4

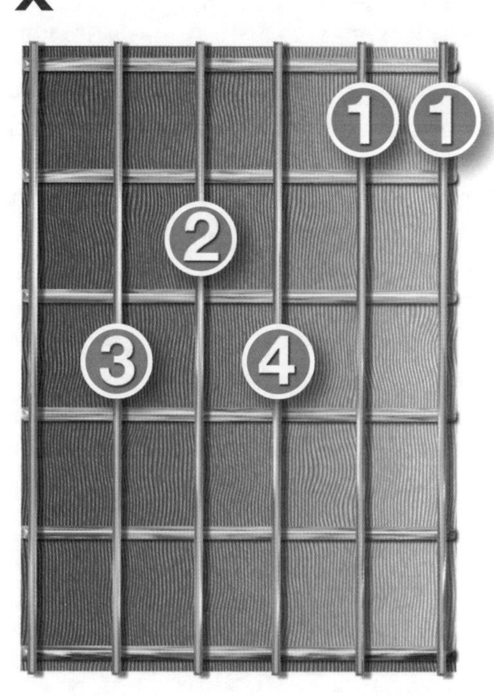

Chord Spelling

1st (E♭), 3rd (G), 5th (B♭), ♭7th (D♭), 9th (F), 11th (A♭)

E♭13

Dominant 13th

(1st position)

5

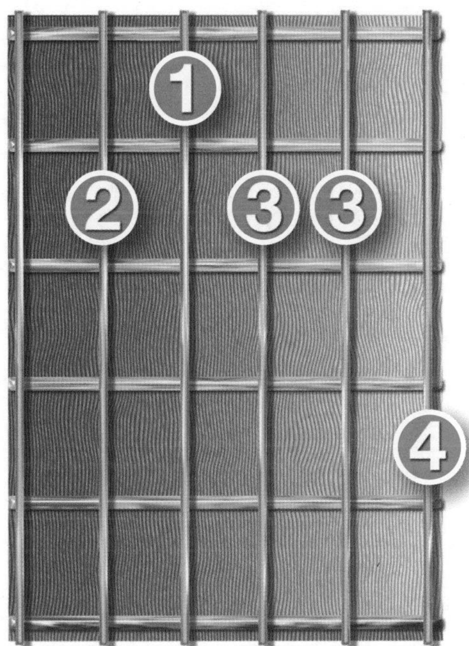

Chord Spelling

1st (E♭), 3rd (G), 5th (B♭), ♭7th (D♭),
9th (F), 11th (A♭), 13th (C)

A
B♭/A♯
B
C
C♯/D♭
D
E♭/D♯
E
F
F♯/G♭
G
A♭/G♯
Other Chords

E♭add9

Major add 9th

(1st position)

3

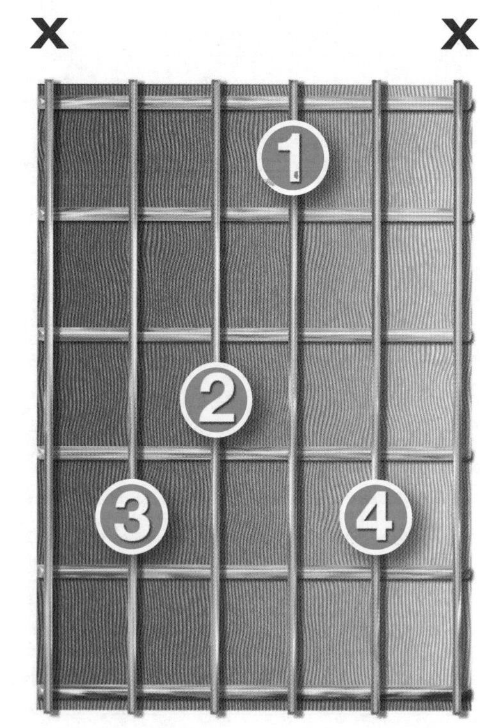

Chord Spelling

1st (E♭), 3rd (G), 5th (B♭),
9th (F)

E♭m9

Minor 9th

(1st position)

Chord Spelling

1st (E♭), ♭3rd (G♭), 5th (B♭), ♭7th (D♭), 9th (F)

E♭maj9

Major 9th

(1st position)

5

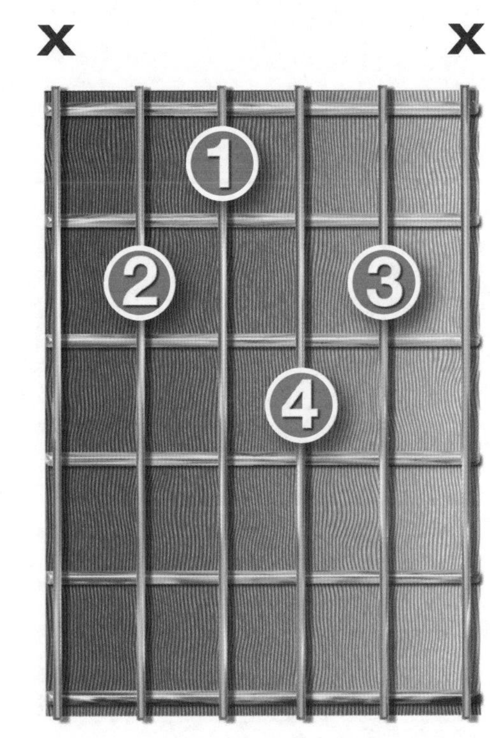

Chord Spelling

1st (E♭), 3rd (G), 5th (B♭), 7th (D), 9th (F)

E♭+

Augmented

(1st position)

Chord Spelling

1st (E♭), 3rd (G), ♯5th (B)

A
B♭/A♯
B
C
C♯/D♭
D
E♭/D♯
E
F
F♯/G♭
G
A♭/G♯
Other Chords

A
B♭/A♯
B
C
C♯/D♭
D
E♭/D♯
E
F
F♯/G♭
G
A♭/G♯
Other Chords

E♭°7

Diminished 7th

(1st position)

Chord Spelling

1st (E♭), ♭3rd (G♭), ♭5th (B♭♭), ♭♭7th (D♭♭)

E♭°

Diminished Triad

(1st position)

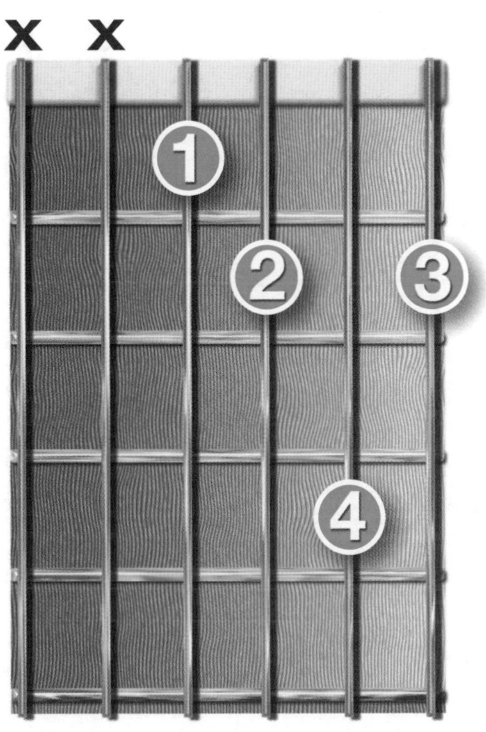

Chord Spelling

1st (E♭), ♭3rd (G♭), ♭5th (B♭♭)

A
B♭/A♯
B
C
C♯/D♭
D
E♭/D♯
E
F
F♯/G♭
G
A♭/G♯
Other Chords

E

Major

(1st position)

Chord Spelling

1st (E), 3rd (G♯), 5th (B)

E

Major

(2nd position)

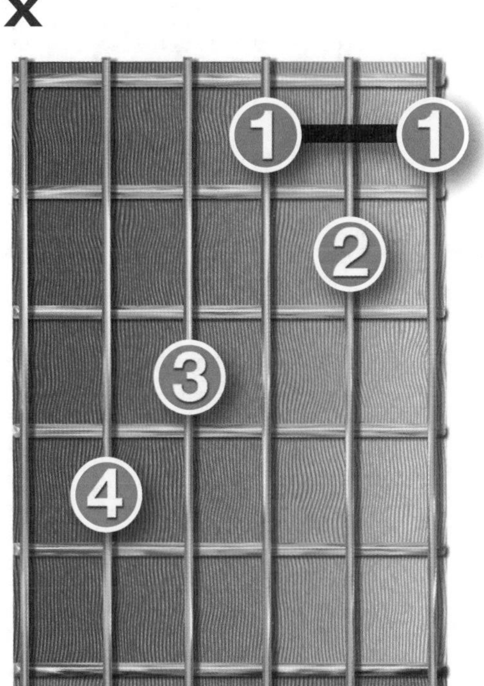

Chord Spelling

1st (E), 3rd (G♯), 5th (B)

A
B♭/A♯
B
C
C♯/D♭
D
E♭/D♯
E
F
F♯/G♭
G
A♭/G♯
Other Chords

Em

Minor

(1st position)

Chord Spelling

1st (E), ♭3rd (G), 5th (B)

Em

Minor

(2nd position)

2

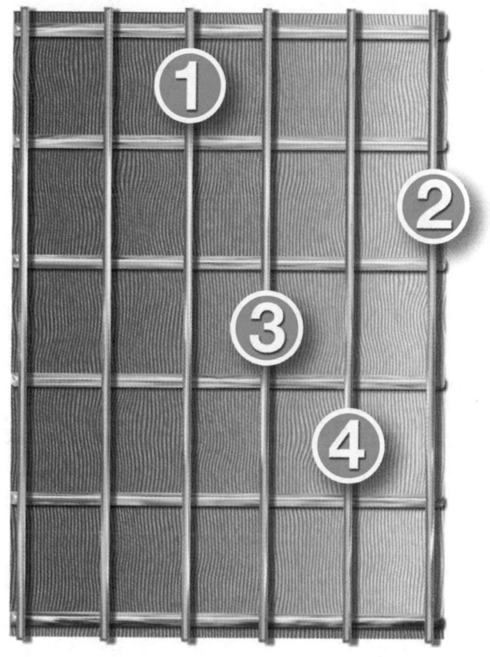

Chord Spelling

1st (E), ♭3rd (G), 5th (B)

Emaj7

Major 7th

(1st position)

Chord Spelling

1st (E), 3rd (G♯), 5th (B), 7th (D♯)

Emaj7

Major 7th

(2nd position)

X X

2

Chord Spelling

1st (E), 3rd (G♯), 5th (B), 7th (D♯)

Em7

Minor 7th

(1st position)

Chord Spelling

1st (E), ♭3rd (G), 5th (B), ♭7th (D)

Em7

Minor 7th

(2nd position)

Chord Spelling

1st (E), ♭3rd (G), 5th (B), ♭7th (D)

Esus4

Suspended 4th

(1st position)

Chord Spelling

1st (E), 4th (A), 5th (B)

Esus4

Suspended 4th

(2nd position)

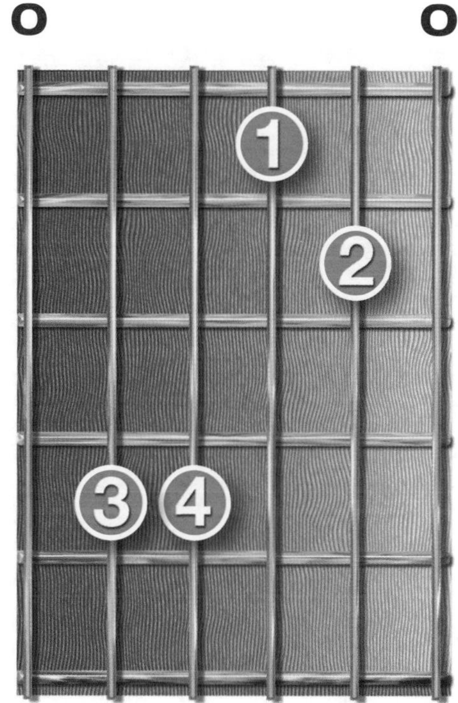

Chord Spelling

1st (E), 4th (A), 5th (B)

A
B♭/A♯
B
C
C♯/D♭
D
E♭/D♯
E
F
F♯/G♭
G
A♭/G♯
Other Chords

E7sus4

Dominant 7th Suspended 4th

(1st position)

Chord Spelling

1st (E), 4th (A), 5th (B), ♭7th (D)

E7sus4

Dominant 7th Suspended 4th

(2nd position)

X X

2

Chord Spelling

1st (E), 4th (A), 5th (B), ♭7th (D)

A
B♭/A♯
B
C
C♯/D♭
D
E♭/D♯
E
F
F♯/G♭
G
A♭/G♯
Other Chords

E6

Major 6th

(1st position)

Chord Spelling

1st (E), 3rd (G♯), 5th (B), 6th (C♯)

E6

Major 6th

(2nd position)

Chord Spelling

1st (E), 3rd (G♯), 5th (B), 6th (C♯)

A
B♭/A♯
B
C
C♯/D♭
D
E♭/D♯
E
F
F♯/G♭
G
A♭/G♯
Other Chords

Em6

Minor 6th

(1st position)

Chord Spelling

1st (E), ♭3rd (G), 5th (B), 6th (C♯)

Em6

Minor 6th

(2nd position)

o

5

Chord Spelling

1st (E), ♭3rd (G), 5th (B), 6th (C♯)

A
B♭/A♯
B
C
C♯/D♭
D
E♭/D♯
E
F
F♯/G♭
G
A♭/G♯
Other Chords

A
B♭/A♯
B
C
C♯/D♭
D
E♭/D♯
E
F
F♯/G♭
G
A♭/G♯
Other Chords

E7

Dominant 7th

(1st position)

Chord Spelling

1st (E), 3rd (G♯), 5th (B), ♭7th (D)

E7

Dominant 7th

(2nd position)

Chord Spelling

1st (E), 3rd (G♯), 5th (B), ♭7th (D)

E9

Dominant 9th

(1st position)

Chord Spelling

1st (E), 3rd (G♯), 5th (B), ♭7th (D), 9th (F♯)

E9

Dominant 9th

(2nd position)

Chord Spelling

1st (E), 3rd (G♯), 5th (B), ♭7th (D), 9th (F♯)

A
B♭/A♯
B
C
C♯/D♭
D
E♭/D♯
E
F
F♯/G♭
G
A♭/G♯
Other Chords

E5

5th 'Power Chord'

(1st position)

Chord Spelling

1st (E), 5th (B)

E6add9

Major 6th add 9th

(1st position)

Chord Spelling

1st (E), 3rd (G♯), 5th (B), 6th (C♯),
9th (F♯)

E11

Dominant 11th

(1st position)

Chord Spelling

1st (E), 3rd (G♯), 5th (B), ♭7th (D),
9th (F♯), 11th (A)

E13

Dominant 13th

(1st position)

Chord Spelling

1st (E), ♭3rd (G), 5th (B), ♭7th (D), 9th (F♯), 11th (A), 13th (C♯)

A
B♭/A♯
B
C
C♯/D♭
D
E♭/D♯
E
F
F♯/G♭
G
A♭/G♯
Other Chords

Eadd9

Major add 9th

(1st position)

Chord Spelling

1st (E), 3rd (G♯), 5th (B), 9th (F♯)

Em9

Minor 9th

(1st position)

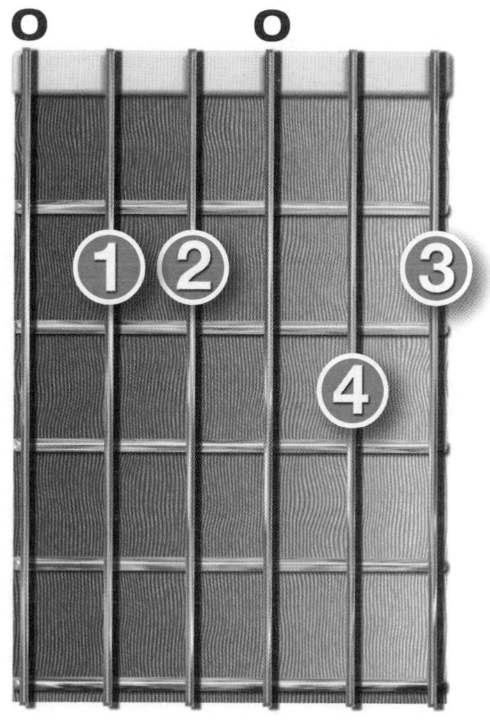

Chord Spelling

1st (E), ♭3rd (G), 5th (B), ♭7th (D), 9th (F♯)

A
B♭/A♯
B
C
C♯/D♭
D
E♭/D♯
E
F
F♯/G♭
G
A♭/G♯
Other Chords

Emaj9

Major 9th

(1st position)

Chord Spelling

1st (E), 3rd (G♯), 5th (B), 7th (D♯), 9th (F♯)

E+

Augmented

(1st position)

Chord Spelling

1st (E), 3rd (G♯), ♯5th (B♯)

A
B♭/A♯
B
C
C♯/D♭
D
E♭/D♯
E
F
F♯/G♭
G
A♭/G♯
Other Chords

E°7

Diminished 7th

(1st position)

Chord Spelling

1st (E), ♭3rd (G), ♭5th (B♭), ♭♭7th (D♭)

E^0

Diminished Triad

(1st position)

Chord Spelling

1st (E), ♭3rd (G), ♭5th (B♭)

A
B♭/A♯
B
C
C♯/D♭
D
E♭/D♯
E
F
F♯/G♭
G
A♭/G♯
Other Chords

F

Major

(1st position)

Chord Spelling

1st (F), 3rd (A), 5th (C)

F

Major

(2nd position)

5

Chord Spelling

1st (F), 3rd (A), 5th (C)

A
B♭/A♯
B
C
C♯/D♭
D
E♭/D♯
E
F
F♯/G♭
G
A♭/G♯
Other Chords

Fm

Minor

(1st position)

Chord Spelling

1st (F), ♭3rd (A♭), 5th (C)

Fm

Minor

(2nd position)

3

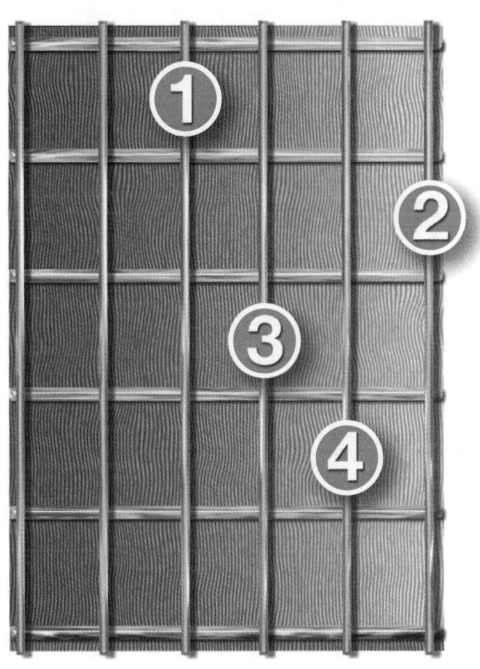

Chord Spelling

1st (F), ♭3rd (A♭), 5th (C)

A
B♭/A♯
B
C
C♯/D♭
D
E♭/D♯
E
F
F♯/G♭
G
A♭/G♯
Other Chords

Fmaj7

Major 7th

(1st position)

Chord Spelling

1st (F), 3rd (A), 5th (C), 7th (E)

Fmaj7

Major 7th

(2nd position)

5

Chord Spelling

1st (F), 3rd (A), 5th (C), 7th (E)

Fm7

Minor 7th

(1st position)

Chord Spelling

1st (F), ♭3rd (A♭), 5th (C), ♭7th (E♭)

Fm7

Minor 7th

(2nd position)

3

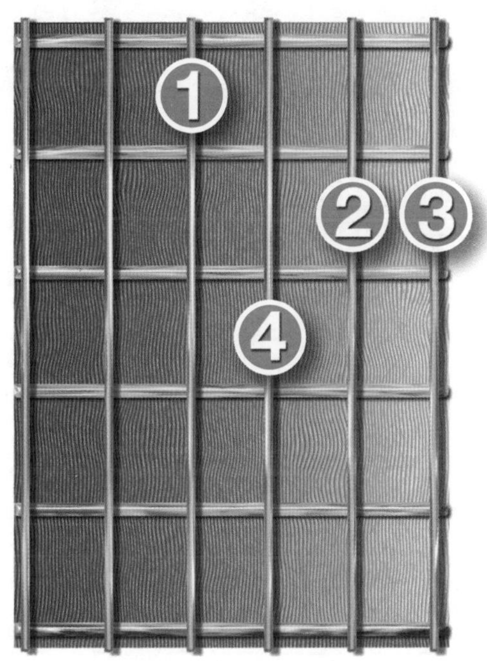

Chord Spelling

1st (F), ♭3rd (A♭), 5th (C), ♭7th (E♭)

A
B♭/A♯
B
C
C♯/D♭
D
E♭/D♯
E
F
F♯/G♭
G
A♭/G♯
Other Chords

Fsus4

Suspended 4th

(1st position)

Chord Spelling

1st (F), 4th (B♭), 5th (C)

Fsus4

Suspended 4th

(2nd position)

5

Chord Spelling

1st (F), 4th (B♭), 5th (C)

A
B♭/A♯
B
C
C♯/D♭
D
E♭/D♯
E
F
F♯/G♭
G
A♭/G♯
Other Chords

F7sus4

Dominant 7th Suspended 4th

(1st position)

Chord Spelling

1st (F), 4th (B♭), 5th (C), ♭7th (E♭)

F7sus4

Dominant 7th Suspended 4th

(2nd position)

3

Chord Spelling

1st (F), 4th (B♭), 5th (C), ♭7th (E♭)

F6

Major 6th

(1st position)

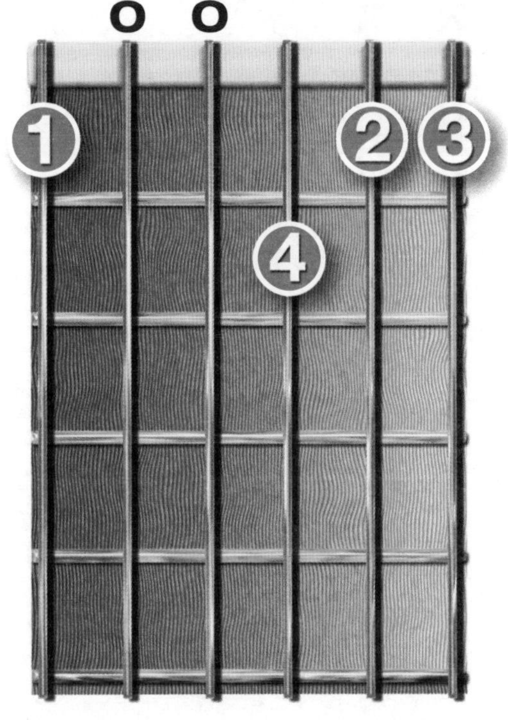

Chord Spelling

1st (F), 3rd (A), 5th (C), 6th (D)

F6

Major 6th

(2nd position)

X X

3

Chord Spelling

1st (F), 3rd (A), 5th (C), 6th (D)

A
B♭/A♯
B
C
C♯/D♭
D
E♭/D♯
E
F
F♯/G♭
G
A♭/G♯
Other Chords

Fm6

Minor 6th

(1st position)

Chord Spelling

1st (F), ♭3rd (A♭), 5th (C), 6th (D)

Fm6

Minor 6th

(2nd position)

6

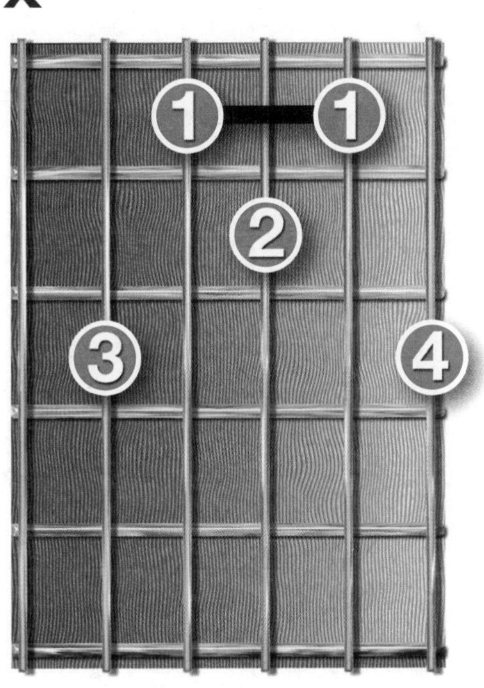

Chord Spelling

1st (F), ♭3rd (A♭), 5th (C), 6th (D)

A
B♭/A♯
B
C
C♯/D♭
D
E♭/D♯
E
F
F♯/G♭
G
A♭/G♯
Other Chords

F7

Dominant 7th

(1st position)

Chord Spelling

1st (F), 3rd (A), 5th (C), ♭7th (E♭)

F7

Dominant 7th

(2nd position)

6

Chord Spelling

1st (F), 3rd (A), 5th (C), ♭7th (E♭)

A
B♭/A♯
B
C
C♯/D♭
D
E♭/D♯
E
F
F♯/G♭
G
A♭/G♯
Other Chords

F9

Dominant 9th

(1st position)

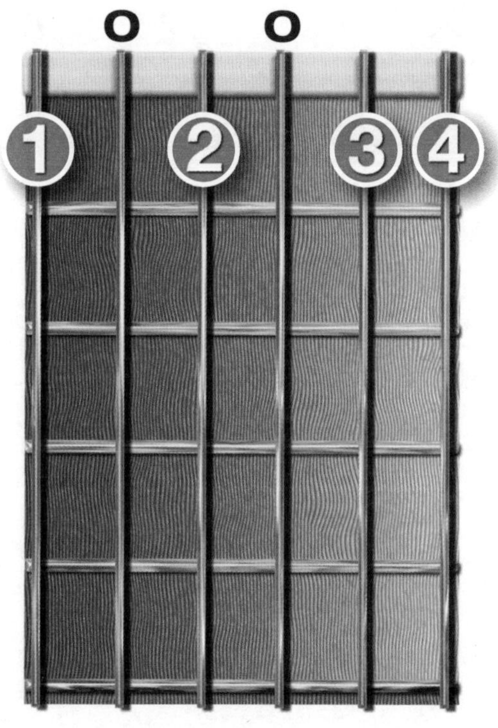

Chord Spelling

1st (F), 3rd (A), 5th (C), ♭7th (E♭), 9th (G)

F9

Dominant 9th

(2nd position)

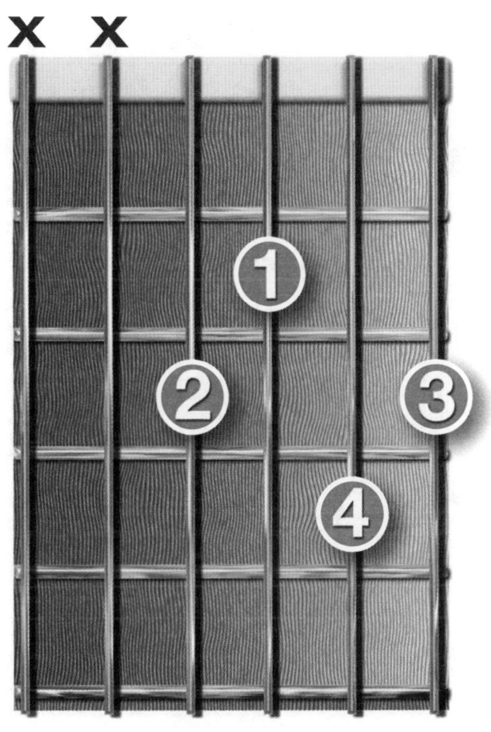

Chord Spelling

1st (F), 3rd (A), 5th (C), ♭7th (E♭),
9th (G)

F5

5th 'Power Chord'

(1st position)

Chord Spelling

1st (F), 5th (C)

F6add9

Major 6th add 9th

(1st position)

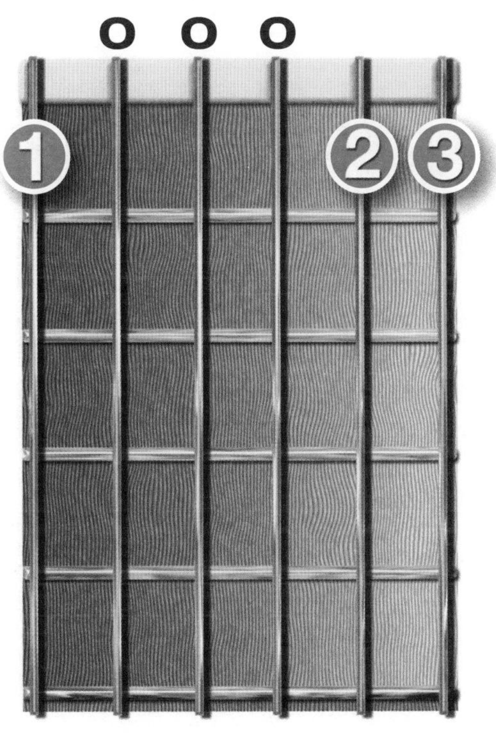

Chord Spelling

1st (F), 3rd (A), 5th (C), 6th (D), 9th (D)

F11

Dominant 11th

(1st position)

6

Chord Spelling

1st (F), 3rd (A), 5th (C), ♭7th (E♭),
9th (G), 11th (B♭)

F13

Dominant 13th

(1st position)

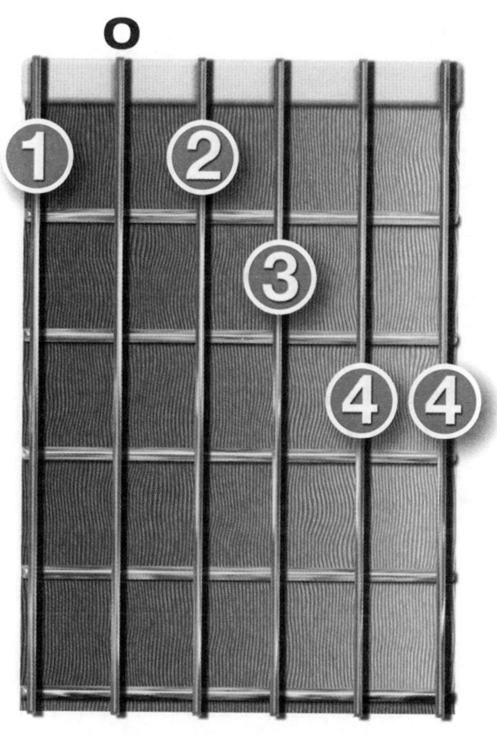

Chord Spelling

1st (F), 3rd (A), 5th (C), ♭7th (E♭), 9th (G), 11th (B♭), 13th (D)

Fadd9

Major add 9th

(1st position)

Chord Spelling

1st (F), 3rd (A), 5th (C),
9th (G)

Fm9

Minor 9th

(1st position)

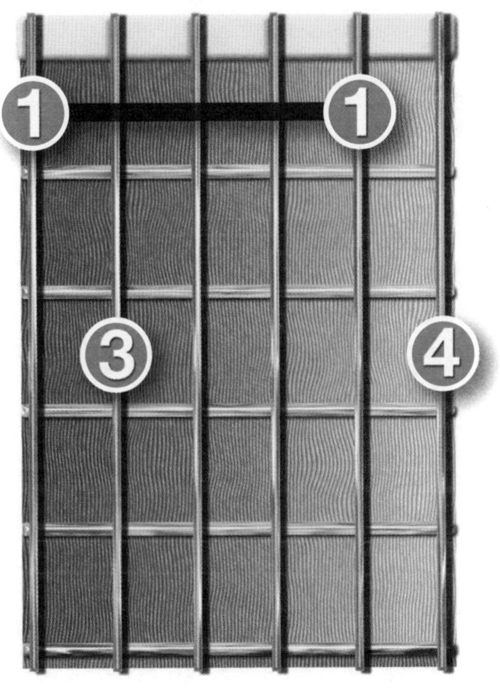

Chord Spelling

1st (F), ♭3rd (A♭), 5th (C), ♭7th (E♭), 9th (G)

Fmaj9

Major 9th

(1st position)

Chord Spelling

1st (F), 3rd (A), 5th (C), 7th (E), 9th (G)

F+

Augmented

(1st position)

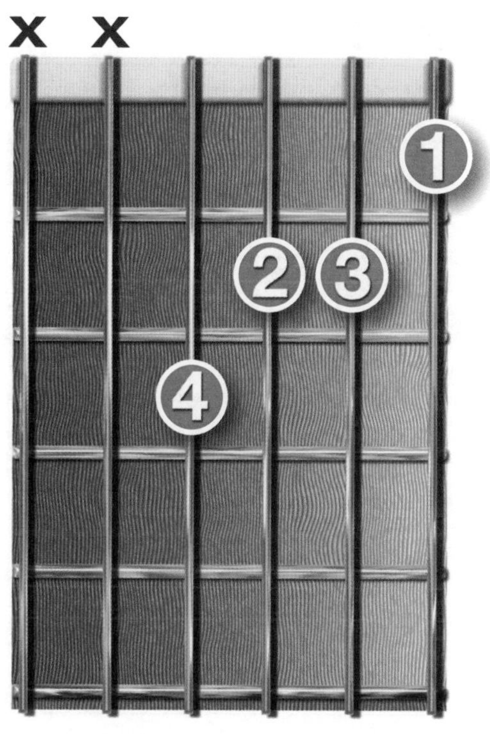

Chord Spelling

1st (F), 3rd (A), ♯5th (C♯)

A
B♭/A♯
B
C
C♯/D♭
D
E♭/D♯
E
F
F♯/G♭
G
A♭/G♯
Other Chords

F°7

Diminished 7th

(1st position)

Chord Spelling

1st (F), ♭3rd (A♭), ♭5th (C♭), ♭♭7th (E♭♭)

F°

Diminished Triad

(1st position)

Chord Spelling

1st (F), ♭3rd (A♭), ♭5th (C♭)

A
B♭/A♯
B
C
C♯/D♭
D
E♭/D♯
E
F
F♯/G♭
G
A♭/G♯
Other Chords

F♯

Major

(1st position)

Chord Spelling

1st (F♯), 3rd (A♯), 5th (C♯)

F♯

Major

(2nd position)

6

Chord Spelling

1st (F♯), 3rd (A♯), 5th (C♯)

F♯m

Minor

(1st position)

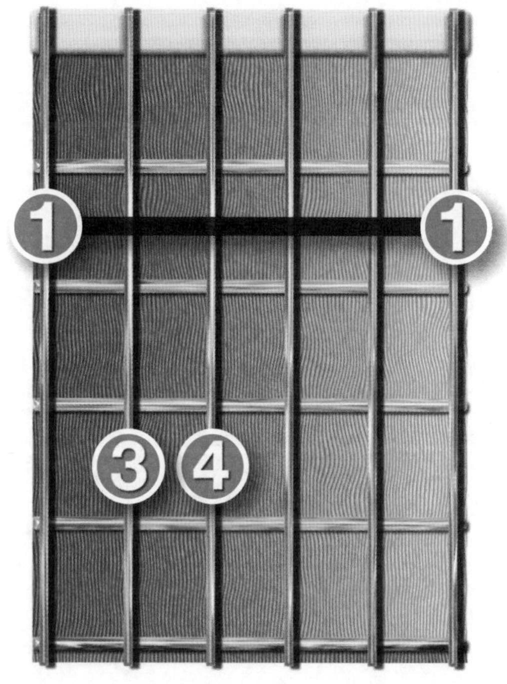

Chord Spelling

1st (F♯), ♭3rd (A), 5th (C♯)

F♯m

Minor

(2nd position)

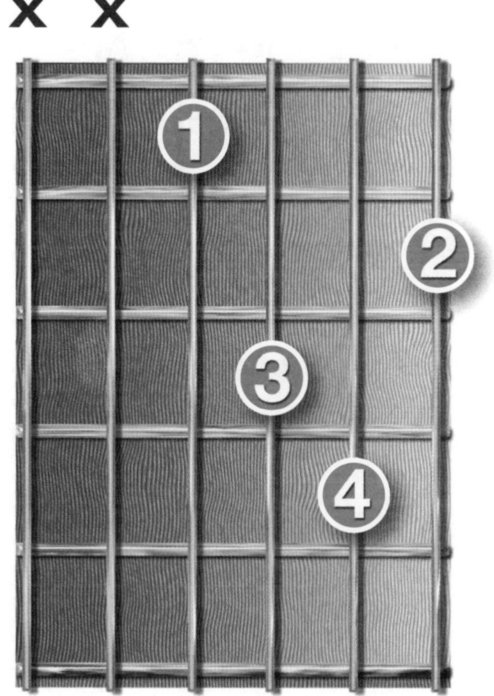

Chord Spelling

1st (F♯), ♭3rd (A), 5th (C♯)

A
B♭/A♯
B
C
C♯/D♭
D
E♭/D♯
E
F
F♯/G♭
G
A♭/G♯
Other Chords

F♯maj7

Major 7th

(1st position)

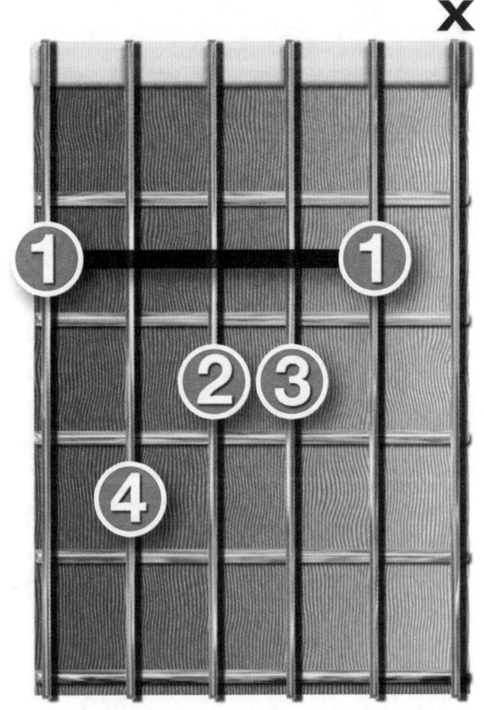

Chord Spelling

1st (F♯), 3rd (A♯), 5th (C♯), 7th (E♯)

F♯maj7

Major 7th

(2nd position)

6

Chord Spelling

1st (F♯), 3rd (A♯), 5th (C♯), 7th (E♯)

A
B♭/A♯
B
C
C♯/D♭
D
E♭/D♯
E
F
F♯/G♭
G
A♭/G♯
Other Chords

F♯m7

Minor 7th

(1st position)

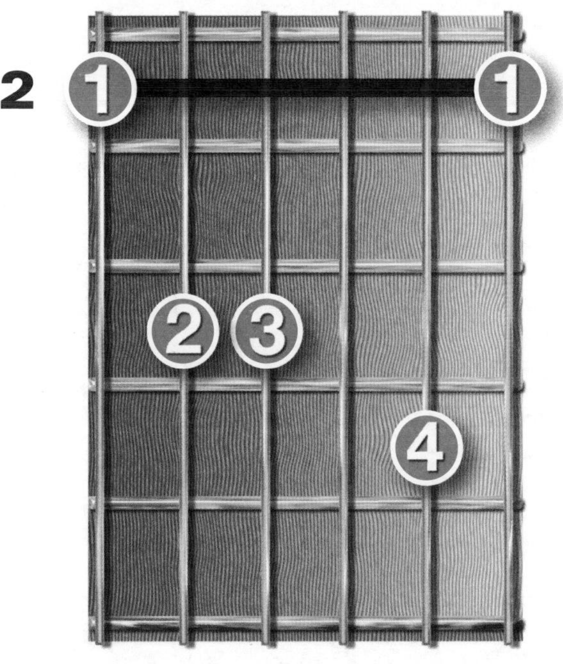

Chord Spelling

1st (F♯), ♭3rd (A), 5th (C♯), ♭7th (E)

F♯m7

Minor 7th

(2nd position)

4

Chord Spelling

1st (F♯), ♭3rd (A), 5th (C♯), ♭7th (E)

F♯sus4

Suspended 4th

(1st position)

Chord Spelling

1st (F♯), 4th (B), 5th (C♯)

F♯sus4

Suspended 4th

(2nd position)

6

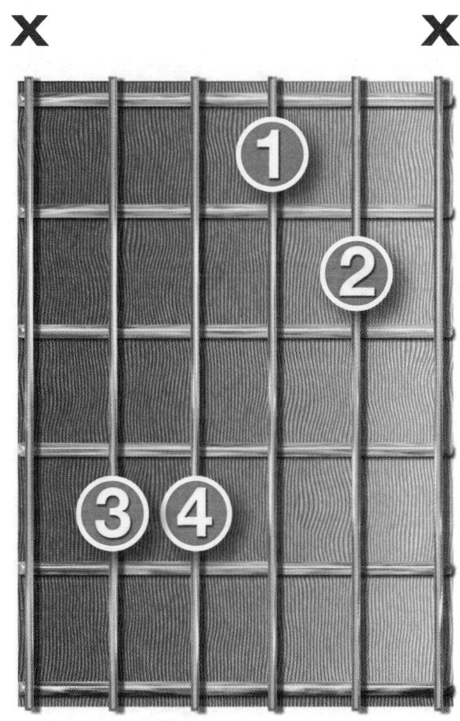

Chord Spelling

1st (F♯), 4th (B), 5th (C♯)

A
B♭/A♯
B
C
C♯/D♭
D
E♭/D♯
E
F
F♯/G♭
G
A♭/G♯
Other Chords

F♯7sus4

Dominant 7th Suspended 4th

(1st position)

Chord Spelling

1st (F♯), 4th (B), 5th (C♯), ♭7th (E)

F♯7sus4

Dominant 7th Suspended 4th

(2nd position)

4

Chord Spelling

1st (F♯), 4th (B), 5th (C♯), ♭7th (E)

A
B♭/A♯
B
C
C♯/D♭
D
E♭/D♯
E
F
F♯/G♭
G
A♭/G♯
Other Chords

F♯6

Major 6th

(1st position)

Chord Spelling

1st (F♯), 3rd (A♯), 5th (C♯), 6th (D♯)

F♯6

Major 6th

(2nd position)

4

Chord Spelling

1st (F♯), 3rd (A♯), 5th (C♯), 6th (D♯)

F♯m6

Minor 6th

(1st position)

Chord Spelling

1st (F♯), ♭3rd (A), 5th (C♯), 6th (D♯)

F♯m6

Minor 6th

(2nd position)

7

Chord Spelling

1st (F♯), ♭3rd (A), 5th (C♯), 6th (D♯)

A
B♭/A♯
B
C
C♯/D♭
D
E♭/D♯
E
F
F♯/G♭
G
A♭/G♯
Other Chords

F♯7

Dominant 7th

(1st position)

Chord Spelling

1st (F♯), 3rd (A♯), 5th (C♯), ♭7th (E)

F♯7

Dominant 7th

(2nd position)

Chord Spelling

1st (F♯), 3rd (A♯), 5th (C♯), ♭7th (E)

F♯9

Dominant 9th

(1st position)

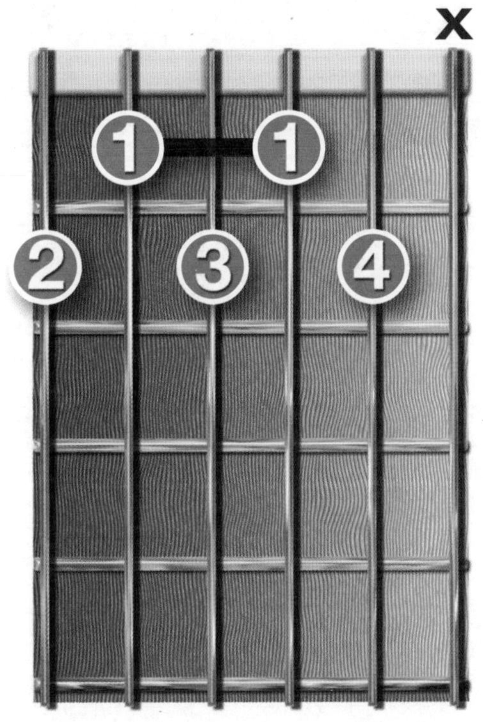

Chord Spelling

1st (F♯), 3rd (A♯), 5th (C♯), ♭7th (E), 9th (G♯)

F♯9

Dominant 9th

(2nd position)

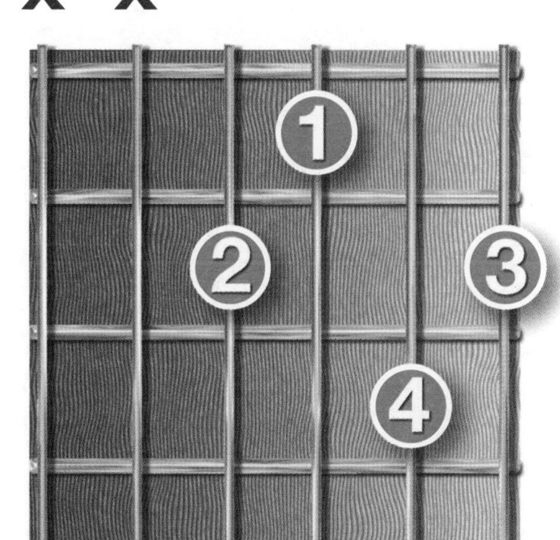

Chord Spelling

1st (F♯), 3rd (A♯), 5th (C♯), ♭7th (E), 9th (G♯)

A
B♭/A♯
B
C
C♯/D♭
D
E♭/D♯
E
F
F♯/G♭
G
A♭/G♯
Other Chords

F♯5

5th 'Power Chord'

(1st position)

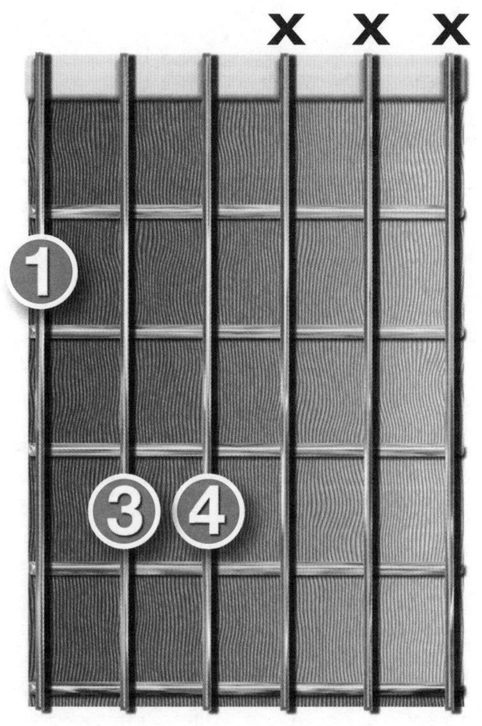

Chord Spelling

1st (F♯), 5th (C♯)

F♯6add9

Major 6th add 9th

(1st position)

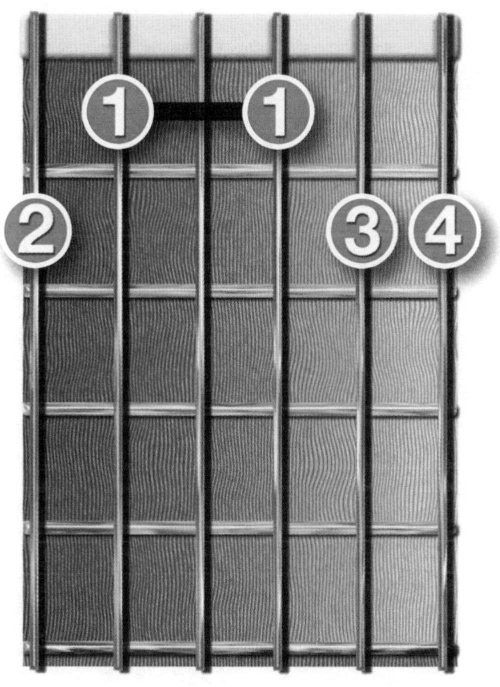

Chord Spelling

1st (F♯), 3rd (A♯), 5th (C♯), 6th (G♯), 9th (D♯)

A
B♭/A♯
B
C
C♯/D♭
D
E♭/D♯
E
F
F♯/G♭
G
A♭/G♯
Other Chords

F♯11

Dominant 11th

(1st position)

2

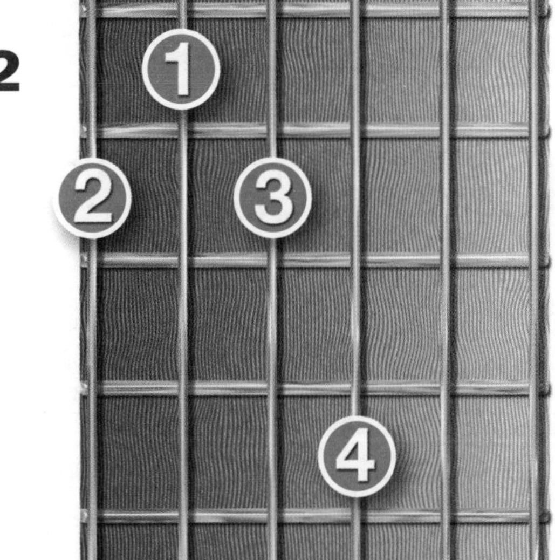

Chord Spelling

1st (F♯), 3rd (A♯), 5th (C♯), ♭7th (E),
9th (G♯), 11th (B)

F♯13

Dominant 13th

(1st position)

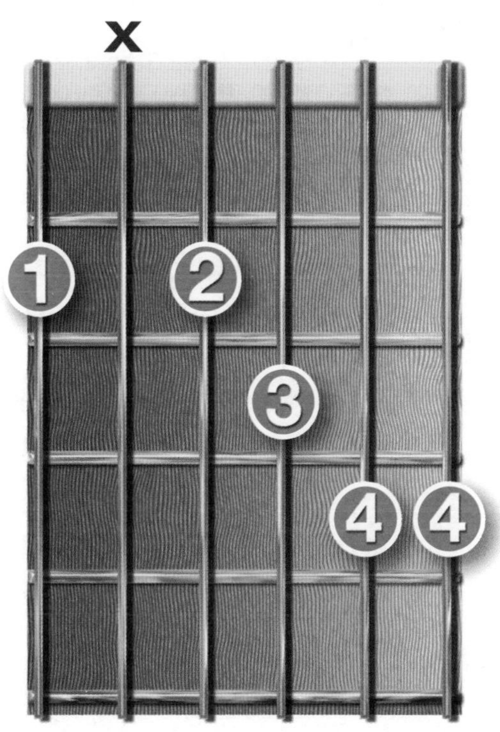

Chord Spelling

1st (F♯), 3rd (A♯), 5th (C♯), ♭7th (E),
9th (G♯), 11th (B), 13th (D♯)

F♯add9

Major add 9th

(1st position)

2

Chord Spelling

1st (F♯), 3rd (A♯), 5th (C♯), 9th (G♯)

F♯m9

Minor 9th

(1st position)

Chord Spelling

1st (F♯), ♭3rd (A), 5th (C♯), ♭7th (E),
9th (G♯)

F♯maj9

Major 9th

(1st position)

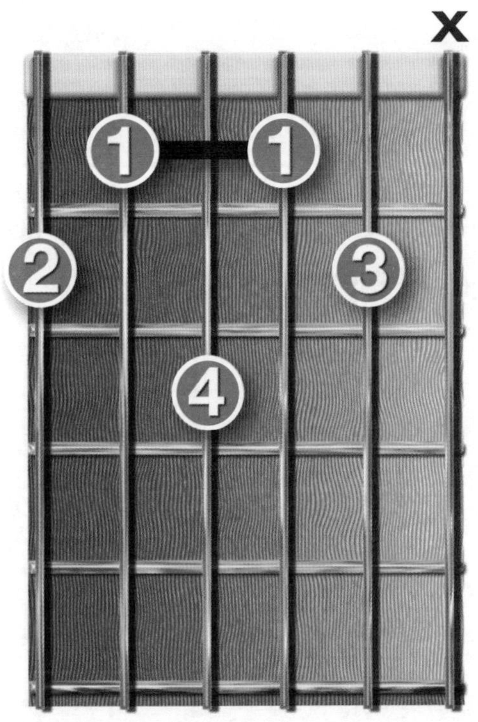

Chord Spelling

1st (F♯), 3rd (A♯), 5th (C♯), 7th (E♯), 9th (G♯)

F♯+

Augmented

(1st position)

2

Chord Spelling

1st (F♯), 3rd (A♯), ♯5th (Cx)

F♯°7

Diminished 7th

(1st position)

Chord Spelling

1st (F♯), ♭3rd (A), ♭5th (C), 𝄫7th (E♭)

F♯⁰

Diminished Triad

(1st position)

Chord Spelling

1st (F♯), ♭3rd (A), ♭5th (C)

G

Major

(1st position)

Chord Spelling

1st (G), 3rd (B), 5th (D)

G

Major

(2nd position)

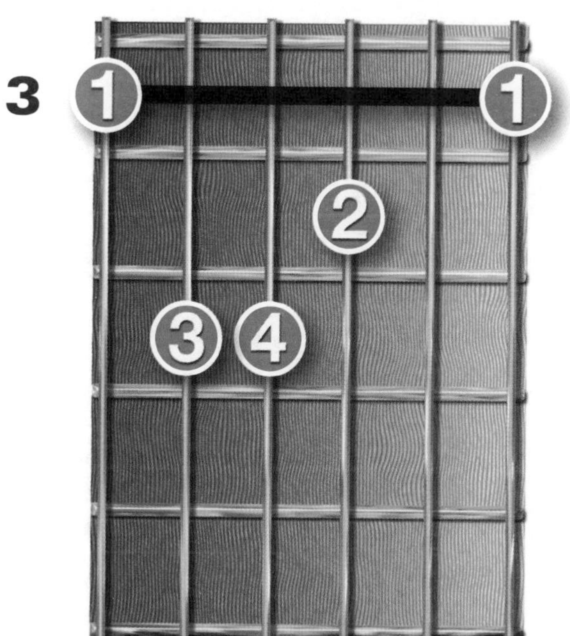

Chord Spelling

1st (G), 3rd (B), 5th (D)

A
B♭/A♯
B
C
C♯/D♭
D
E♭/D♯
E
F
F♯/G♭
G
A♭/G♯
Other Chords

Gm

Minor

(1st position)

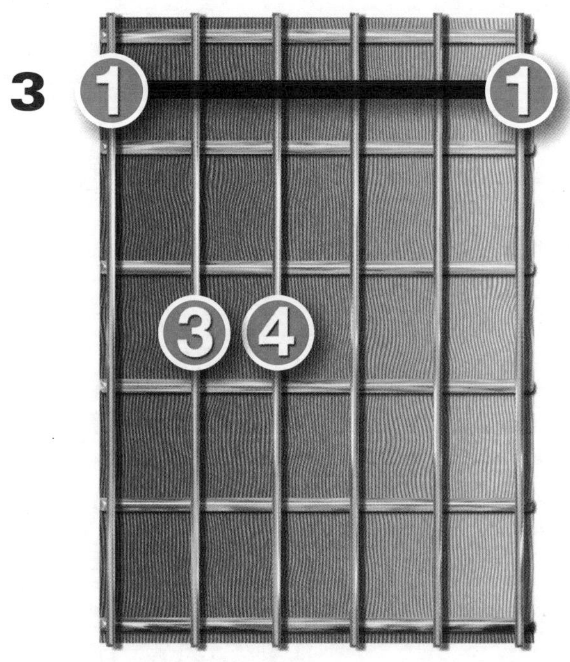

Chord Spelling

1st (G), ♭3rd (B♭), 5th (D)

Gm

Minor

(2nd position)

5

Chord Spelling

1st (G), ♭3rd (B♭), 5th (D)

A
B♭/A♯
B
C
C♯/D♭
D
E♭/D♯
E
F
F♯/G♭
G
A♭/G♯
Other Chords

Gmaj7

Major 7th

(1st position)

x x

2

Chord Spelling

1st (G), 3rd (B), 5th (D), 7th (F♯)

Gmaj7

Major 7th

(2nd position)

7

Chord Spelling

1st (G), 3rd (B), 5th (D), 7th (F♯)

A
B♭/A♯
B
C
C♯/D♭
D
E♭/D♯
E
F
F♯/G♭
G
A♭/G♯
Other Chords

Gm7

Minor 7th

(1st position)

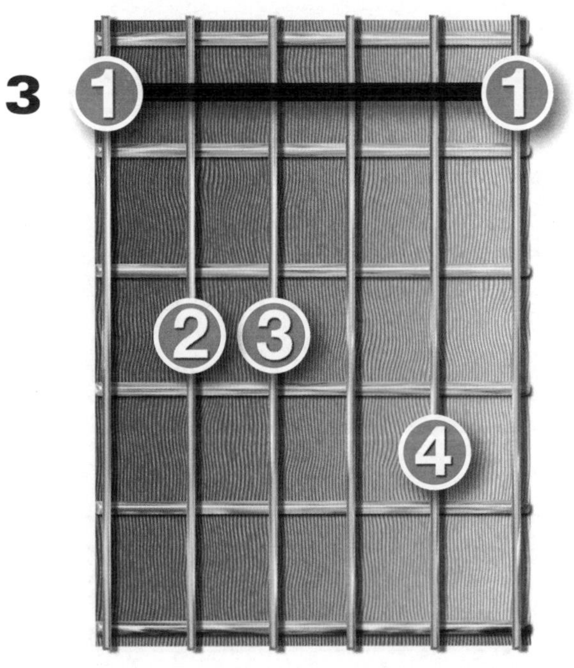

Chord Spelling

1st (G), ♭3rd (B♭), 5th (D), ♭7th (F)

Gm7

Minor 7th

(2nd position)

5

Chord Spelling

1st (G), ♭3rd (B♭), 5th (D), ♭7th (F)

Gsus4

Suspended 4th

(1st position)

Chord Spelling

1st (G), 4th (C), 5th (D)

Gsus4

Suspended 4th

(2nd position)

Chord Spelling

1st (G), 4th (C), 5th (D)

A
B♭/A♯
B
C
C♯/D♭
D
E♭/D♯
E
F
F♯/G♭
G
A♭/G♯
Other Chords

G7sus4

Dominant 7th Suspended 4th

(1st position)

Chord Spelling

1st (G), 4th (C), 5th (D), ♭7th (F)

G7sus4

Dominant 7th Suspended 4th

(2nd position)

Chord Spelling

1st (G), 4th (C), 5th (D), ♭7th (F)

A
B♭/A♯
B
C
C♯/D♭
D
E♭/D♯
E
F
F♯/G♭
G
A♭/G♯
Other Chords

G6

Major 6th

(1st position)

Chord Spelling

1st (G), 3rd (B), 5th (D), 6th (E)

G6

Major 6th

(2nd position)

Chord Spelling

1st (G), 3rd (B), 5th (D), 6th (E)

A
B♭/A♯
B
C
C♯/D♭
D
E♭/D♯
E
F
F♯/G♭
G
A♭/G♯
Other Chords

Gm6

Minor 6th

(1st position)

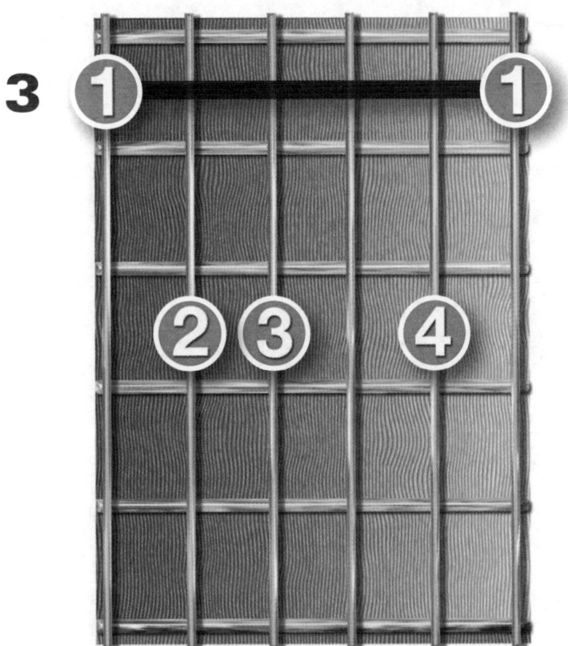

Chord Spelling

1st (G), ♭3rd (B♭), 5th (D), 6th (E)

Gm6

Minor 6th

(2nd position)

x

8

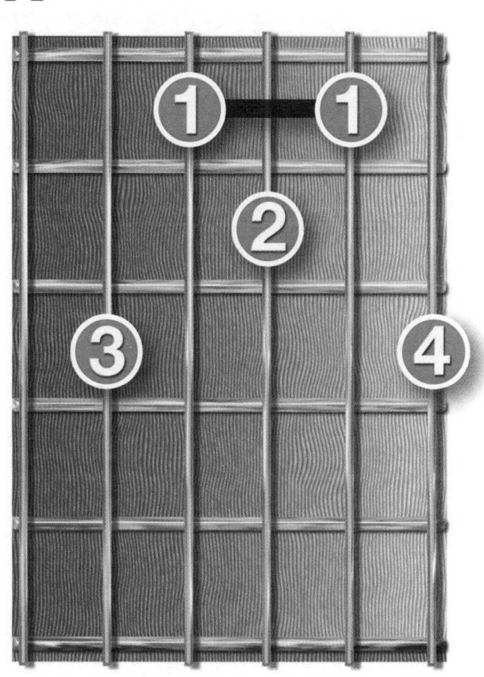

Chord Spelling

1st (G), ♭3rd (B♭), 5th (D), 6th (E)

G7

Dominant 7th

(1st position)

Chord Spelling

1st (G), 3rd (B), 5th (D), ♭7th (F)

G7

Dominant 7th

(2nd position)

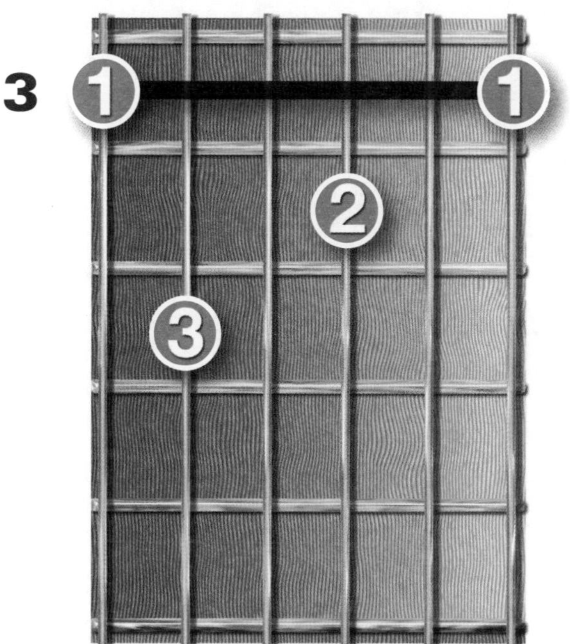

Chord Spelling

1st (G), 3rd (B), 5th (D), ♭7th (F)

B
C
C♯/D♭
D
E♭/D♯
E
F
F♯/G♭
G
A♭/G♯
Other Chords

G9

Dominant 9th

(1st position)

Chord Spelling

1st (G), 3rd (B), 5th (D), ♭7th (F), 9th (A)

G9

Dominant 9th

(2nd position)

4

Chord Spelling

1st (G), 3rd (B), 5th (D), ♭7th (F), 9th (A)

G5

5th 'Power Chord'

(1st position)

x x x

3

Chord Spelling

1st (G), 5th (D)

G6add9

Major 6th add 9th

(1st position)

Chord Spelling

1st (G), 3rd (B), 5th (D), 6th (E), 9th (A)

G11

Dominant 11th

(1st position)

Chord Spelling

1st (G), 3rd (B), 5th (D), ♭7th (F), 9th (A), 11th (C)

G13

Dominant 13th

(1st position)

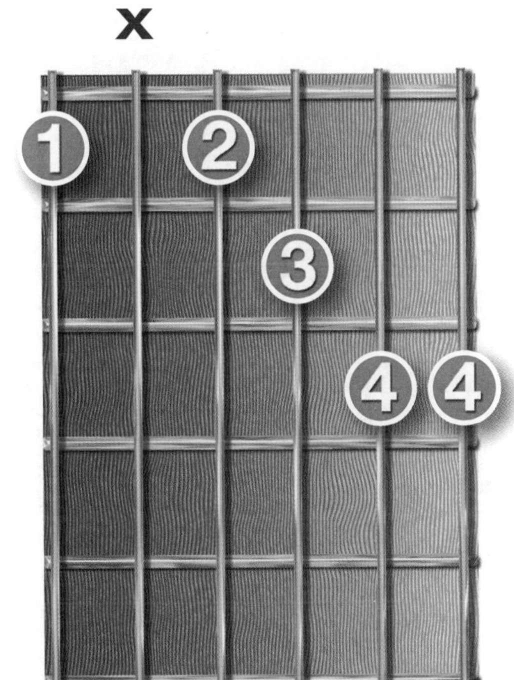

Chord Spelling

1st (G), 3rd (B), 5th (D), ♭7th (F), 9th (A), 11th (C) 13th (E)

A
B♭/A♯
B
C
C♯/D♭
D
E♭/D♯
E
F
F♯/G♭
G
A♭/G♯
Other Chords

Gadd9

Major add 9th

(1st position)

Chord Spelling

1st (G), 3rd (B), 5th (D), 9th (A)

Gm9

Minor 9th

(1st position)

Chord Spelling

1st (G), ♭3rd (B♭), 5th (D), ♭7th (F), 9th (A)

Gmaj9

Major 9th

(1st position)

Chord Spelling

1st (G), 3rd (B), 5th (D), 7th (F♯), 9th (A)

G+

Augmented

(1st position)

3

Chord Spelling

1st (G), 3rd (B), ♯5th (D♯)

G°7

Diminished 7th

(1st position)

Chord Spelling

1st (G), ♭3rd (B♭), ♭5th (D♭), 𝄫7th (F♭)

G^{0}

Diminished Triad

(1st position)

2

Chord Spelling

1st (G), ♭3rd (B♭), ♭5th (D♭)

A♭

Major

(1st position)

Chord Spelling

1st (A♭), 3rd (C), 5th (E♭)

A♭

Major

(2nd position)

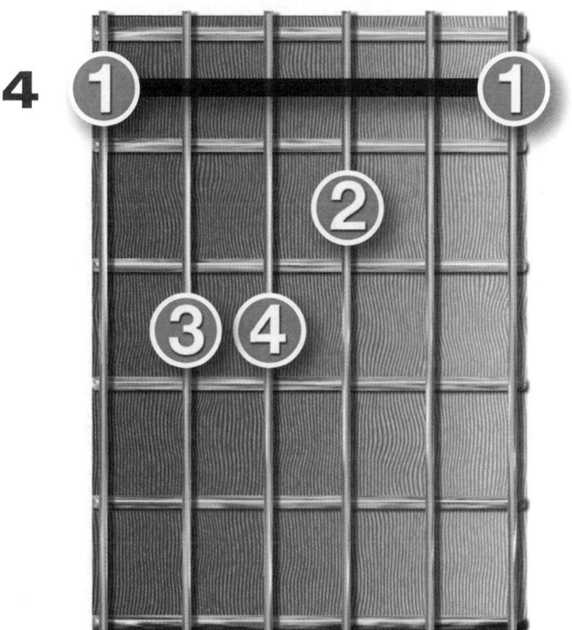

Chord Spelling

1st (A♭), 3rd (C), 5th (E♭)

A
B♭/A♯
B
C
C♯/D♭
D
E♭/D♯
E
F
F♯/G♭
G
A♭/G♯
Other Chords

A
B♭/A♯
B
C
C♯/D♭
D
E♭/D♯
E
F
F♯/G♭
G
A♭/G♯
Other Chords

A♭m

Minor

(1st position)

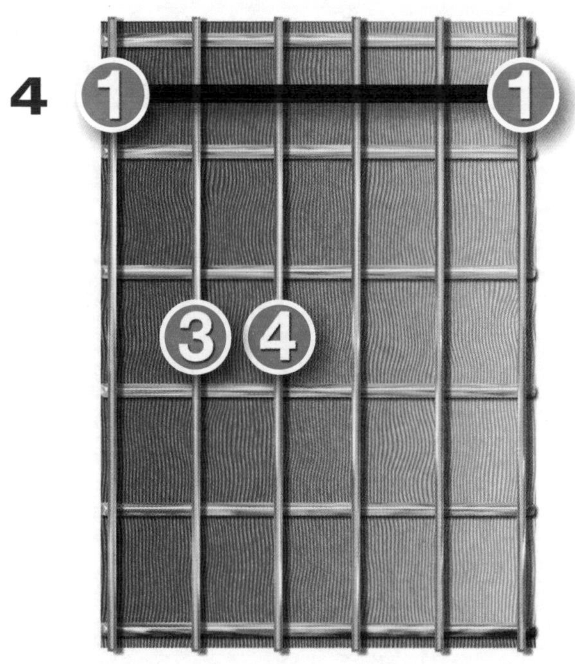

Chord Spelling

1st (A♭), ♭3rd (C♭), 5th (E♭)

A♭m

Minor

(2nd position)

6

Chord Spelling

1st (A♭), ♭3rd (C♭), 5th (E♭)

A♭maj7

Major 7th

(1st position)

3

Chord Spelling

1st (A♭), 3rd (C), 5th (E♭), 7th (G)

A♭maj7

Major 7th

(2nd position)

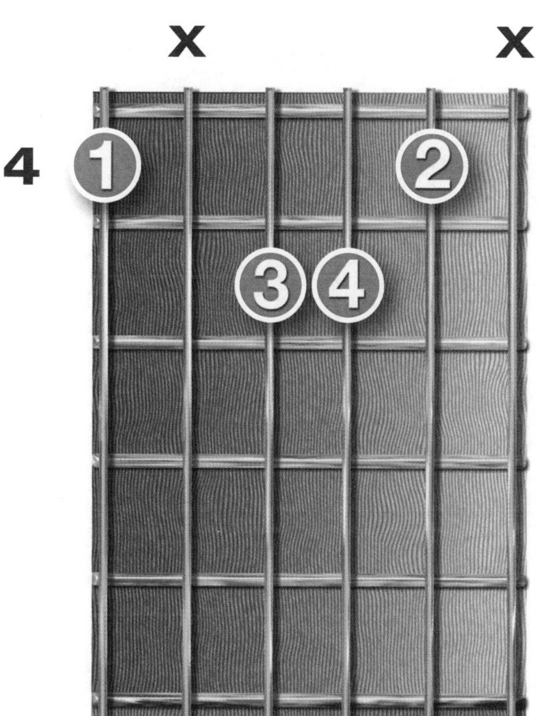

Chord Spelling

1st (A♭), 3rd (C), 5th (E♭), 7th (G)

A
B♭/A♯
B
C
C♯/D♭
D
E♭/D♯
E
F
F♯/G♭
G
A♭/G♯
Other Chords

A♭m7

Minor 7th

(1st position)

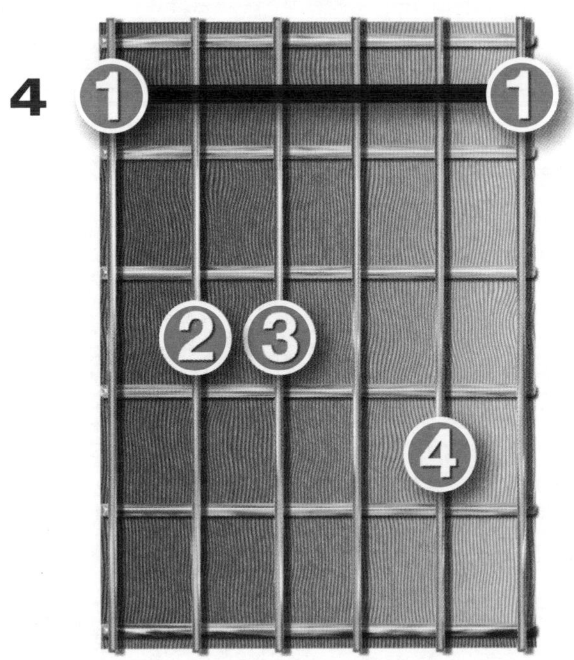

Chord Spelling

1st (A♭), ♭3rd (C♭), 5th (E♭), ♭7th (G♭)

A♭m7

Minor 7th

(2nd position)

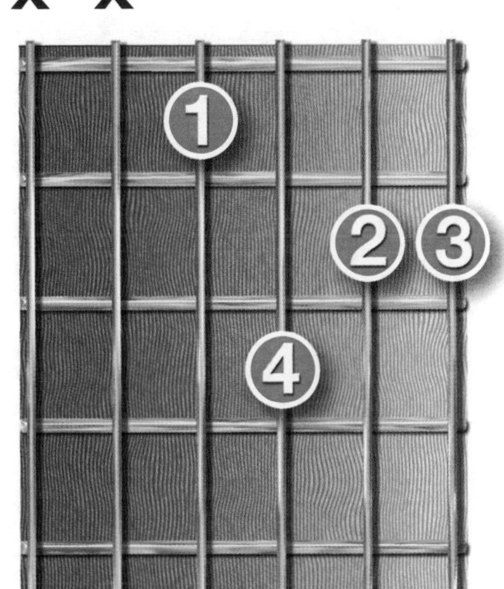

Chord Spelling

1st (A♭), ♭3rd (C♭), 5th (E♭), ♭7th (G♭)

A♭sus4

Suspended 4th

(1st position)

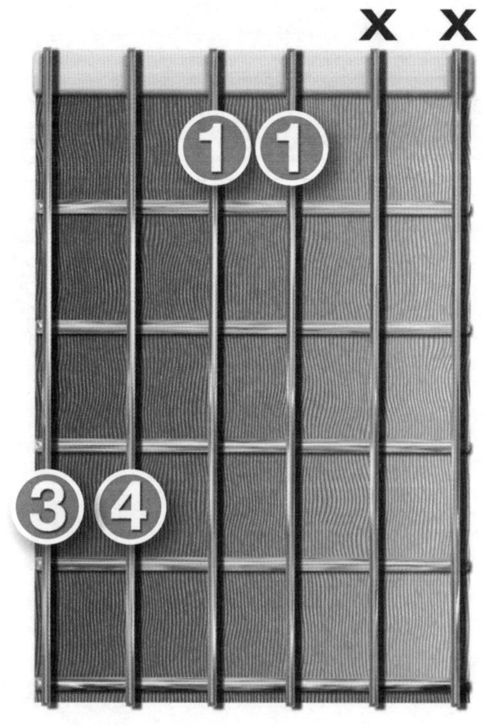

Chord Spelling

1st (A♭), 4th (D♭), 5th (E♭)

A♭sus4

Suspended 4th

(2nd position)

Chord Spelling

1st (A♭), 4th (D♭), 5th (E♭)

A
B♭/A♯
B
C
C♯/D♭
D
E♭/D♯
E
F
F♯/G♭
G
A♭/G♯
Other Chords

A♭7sus4

Dominant 7th Suspended 4th

(1st position)

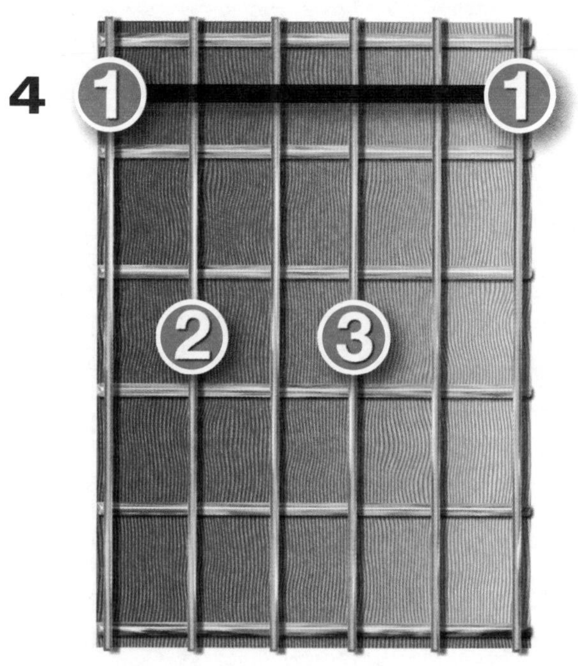

Chord Spelling

1st (A♭), 4th (D♭), 5th (E♭), 7th (G♭)

A♭7sus4

Dominant 7th Suspended 4th

(2nd position)

Chord Spelling

1st (A♭), 4th (D♭), 5th (E♭), 7th (G♭)

A♭6

Major 6th

(1st position)

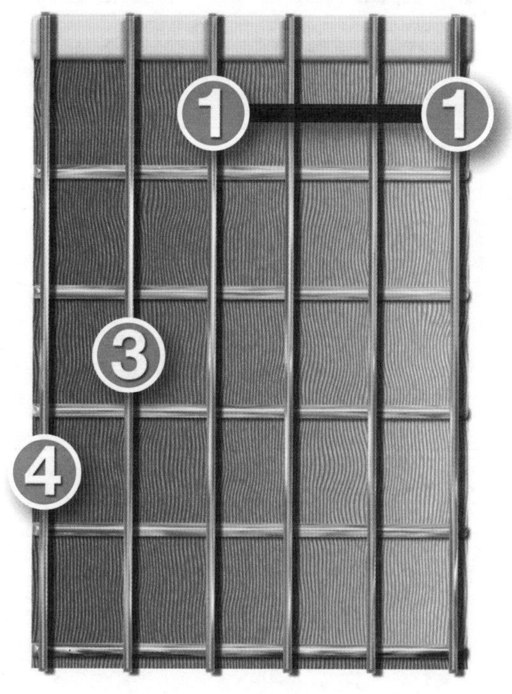

Chord Spelling

1st (A♭), 3rd (C), 5th (E♭), 6th (F)

A♭6

Major 6th

(2nd position)

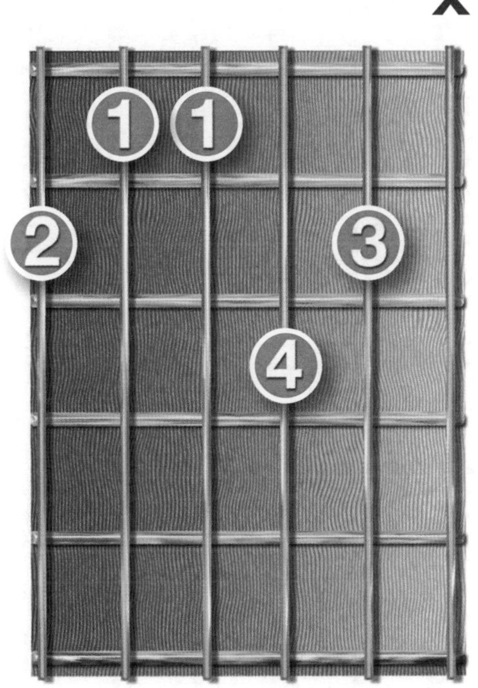

Chord Spelling

1st (A♭), 3rd (C), 5th (E♭), 6th (F)

A
B♭/A♯
B
C
C♯/D♭
D
E♭/D♯
E
F
F♯/G♭
G
A♭/G♯
Other Chords

A♭m6

Minor 6th

(1st position)

Chord Spelling

1st (A♭), ♭3rd (C♭), 5th (E♭), 6th (F)

A♭m6

Minor 6th

(2nd position)

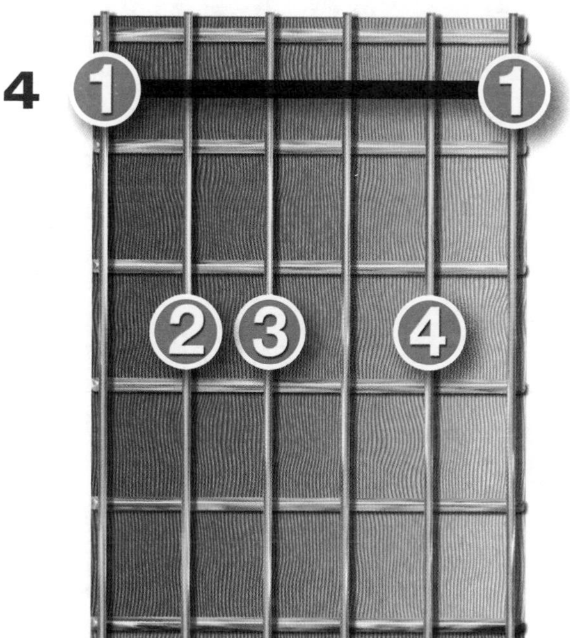

Chord Spelling

1st (A♭), ♭3rd (C♭), 5th (E♭), 6th (F)

A♭7

Dominant 7th

(1st position)

Chord Spelling

1st (A♭), 3rd (C), 5th (E♭), ♭7th (G♭)

A♭7

Dominant 7th

(2nd position)

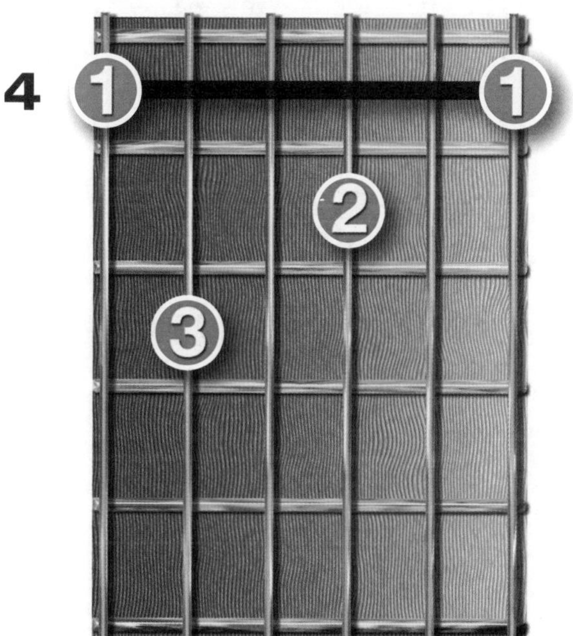

Chord Spelling

1st (A♭), 3rd (C), 5th (E♭), ♭7th (G♭)

A
B♭/A♯
B
C
C♯/D♭
D
E♭/D♯
E
F
F♯/G♭
G
A♭/G♯
Other Chords

A♭9

Dominant 9th

(1st position)

Chord Spelling

1st (A♭), 3rd (C), 5th (E♭), ♭7th (G♭), 9th (B)

A♭9

Dominant 9th

(2nd position)

5

Chord Spelling

1st (A♭), 3rd (C), 5th (E♭), ♭7th (G♭),
9th (B)

A♭5

5th 'Power Chord'

(1st position)

Chord Spelling

1st (A♭), 5th (E♭)

A♭6add9

Major 6th add 9th

(1st position)

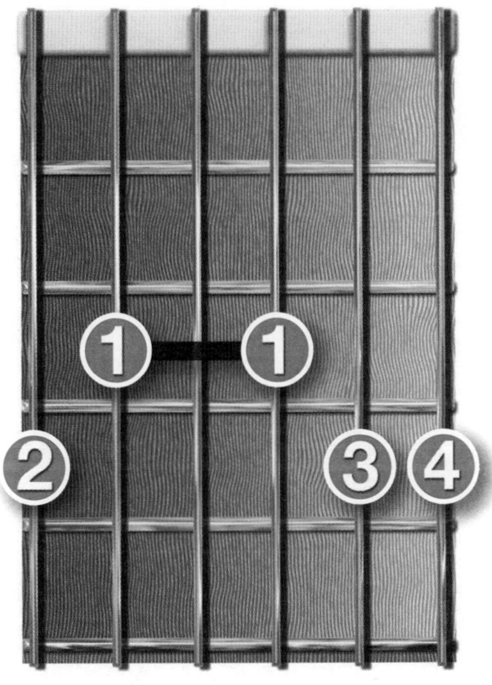

Chord Spelling

1st (A♭), 3rd (C), 5th (E♭), 6th (F), 9th (B♭)

A♭11

Dominant 11th

(1st position)

Chord Spelling

1st (A♭), 3rd (C), 5th (E♭), ♭7th (G♭), 9th (B♭), 11th (D♭)

A♭13

Dominant 13th

(1st position)

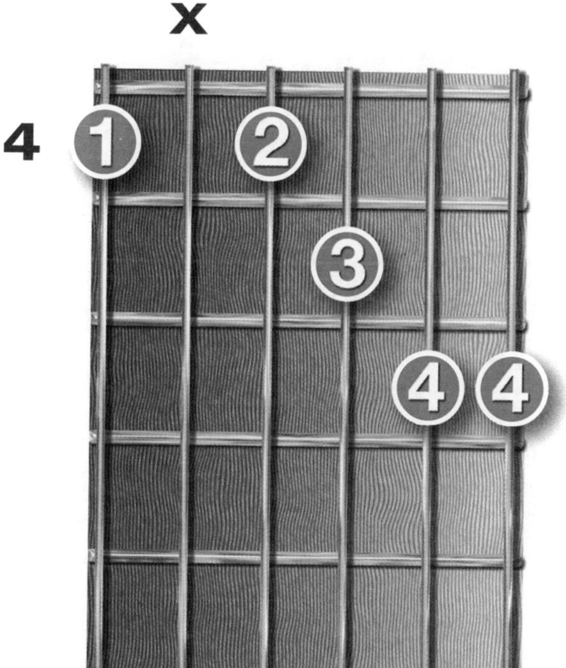

Chord Spelling

1st (A♭), 3rd (C), 5th (E♭), ♭7th (G♭), 9th (B♭), 11th (D♭), 13th (F)

A
B♭/A#
B
C
C#/D♭
D
E♭/D#
E
F
F#/G♭
G
A♭/G#
Other Chords

A♭add9

Major add 9th

(1st position)

Chord Spelling

1st (A♭), 3rd (C), 5th (E♭), 9th (B♭)

A♭m9

Minor 9th

(1st position)

4

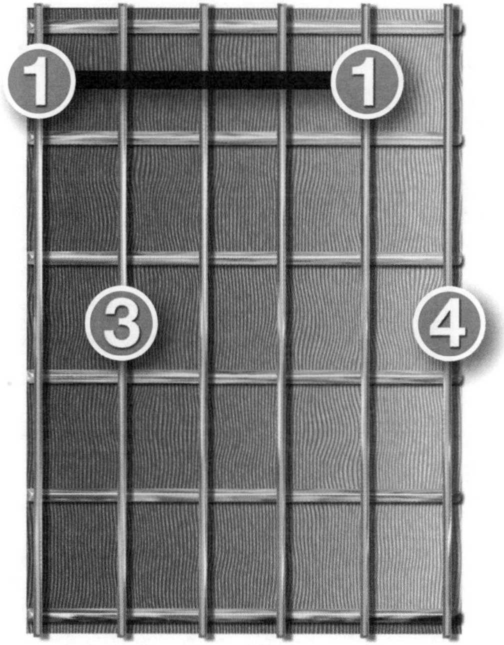

Chord Spelling

1st (A♭), ♭3rd (C♭), 5th (E♭), ♭7th (G♭), 9th (B♭)

A♭maj9

Major 9th

(1st position)

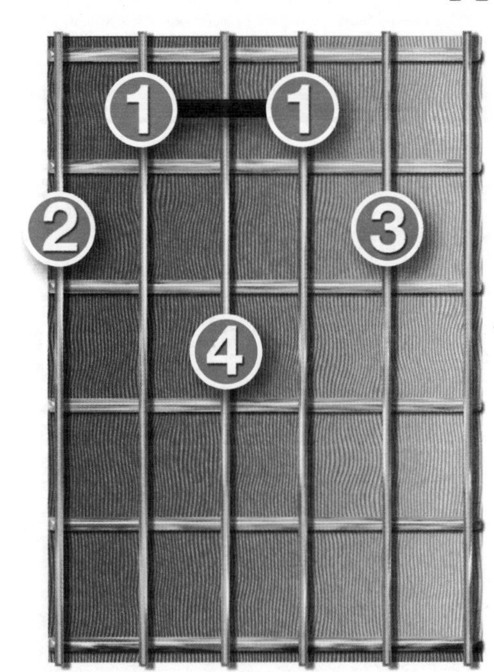

Chord Spelling

1st (A♭), 3rd (C), 5th (E♭), 7th (G), 9th (B♭)

A♭+

Augmented

(1st position)

Chord Spelling

1st (A♭), 3rd (C), ♯5th (E)

A
B♭/A♯
B
C
C♯/D♭
D
E♭/D♯
E
F
F♯/G♭
G
A♭/G♯
Other Chords

A♭°7

Diminished 7th

(1st position)

6

Chord Spelling

1st (A♭), ♭3rd (C♭), ♭5th (E♭♭), ♭♭7th (G♭♭)

A♭°

Diminished Triad

(1st position)

Chord Spelling

1st (A♭), ♭3rd (C♭), ♭5th (E♭♭)

A
B♭/A♯
B
C
C♯/D♭
D
E♭/D♯
E
F
F♯/G♭
G
A♭/G♯
Other Chords

A7$^{\sharp5}$

Dominant 7th Sharpened 5th

(1st position)

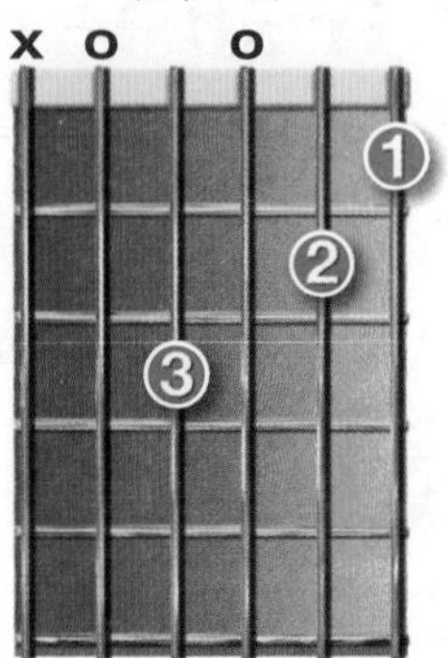

Chord Spelling

1st (A), 3rd (C♯), ♯5th (E♯), ♭7th (G)

A7$^{\sharp9}$

Dominant 7th Sharpened 9th

(1st position)

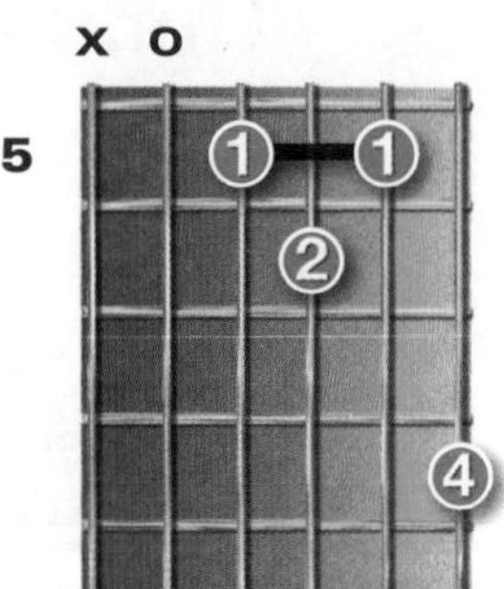

Chord Spelling

1st (A), 3rd (C♯), 5th (E), ♭7th (G), ♯9th (B♯)

A7$^{\flat5}$

Dominant 7th Flattened 5th

(1st position)

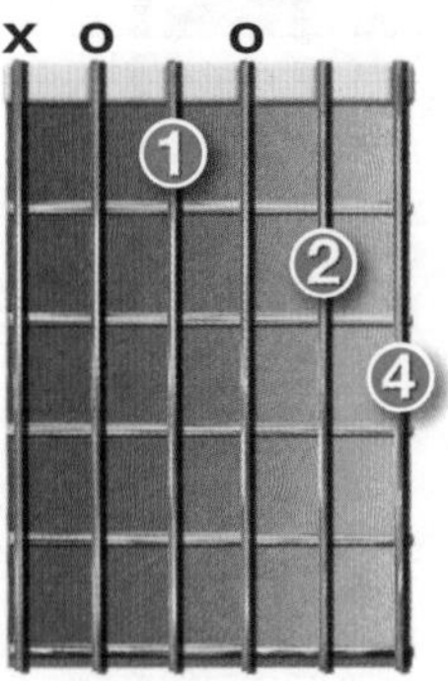

Chord Spelling

1st (A), 3rd (C♯), ♭5th (E♭), ♭7th (G)

A7$^{\flat9}$

Dominant 7th Flattened 9th

(1st position)

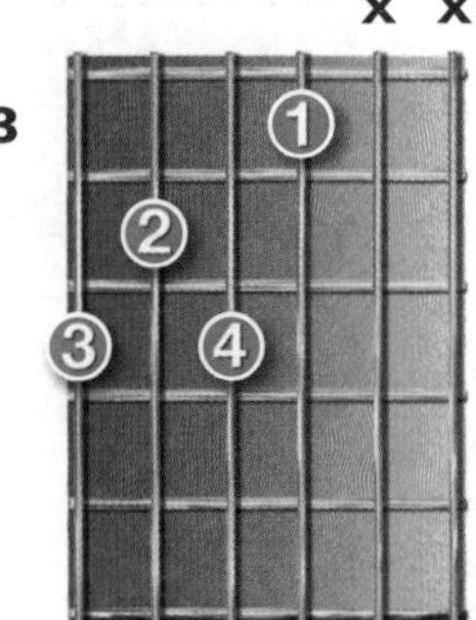

Chord Spelling

1st (A), 3rd (C♯), 5th (E), ♭7th (G), ♭9th (B♭)

A9♭5

Dominant 9th Flattened 5th

(1st position)

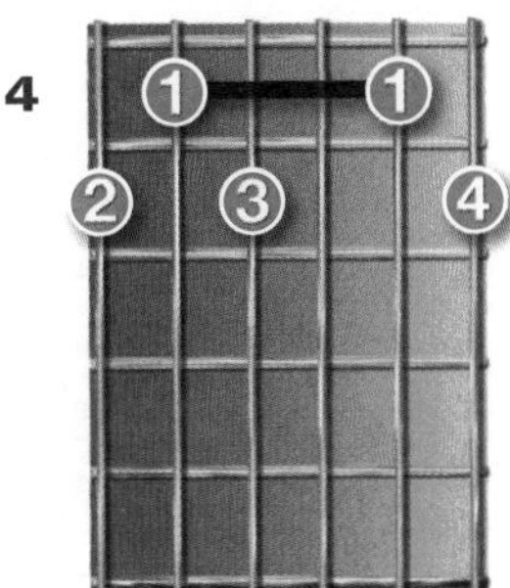

Chord Spelling

1st (A), 3rd (C♯), ♭5th (E♭), ♭7th (G), 9th (B)

B♭7♯5

Dominant 7th Sharpened 5th

(1st position)

Chord Spelling

1st (B♭), 3rd (D), ♯5th (F♯), ♭7th (A♭)

B♭7♯9

Dominant 7th Sharpened 9th

(1st position)

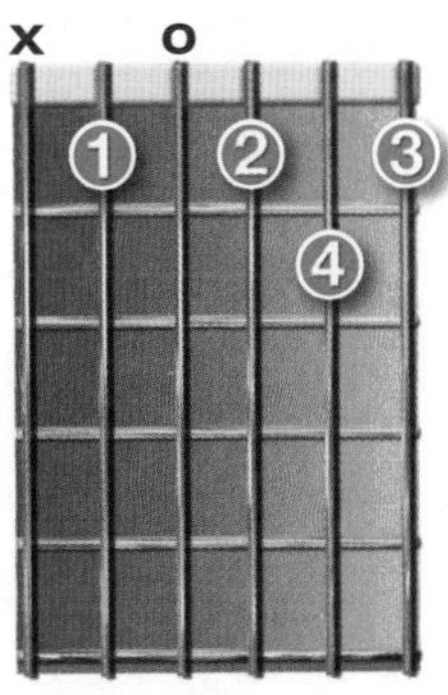

Chord Spelling

1st (B♭), 3rd (D), 5th (F), ♭7th (A♭), ♯9th (C♯)

B♭7♭5

Dominant 7th Flattened 5th

(1st position)

Chord Spelling

1st (B♭), 3rd (D), ♭5th (F♭), ♭7th (A♭)

A
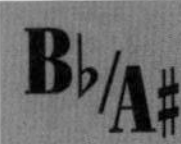

B
C
C♯/D♭
D
E♭/D♯
E
F
F♯/G♭
G
A♭/G♯
Other Chords

B♭7$^{\flat 9}$

Dominant 7th Flattened 9th

(1st position)

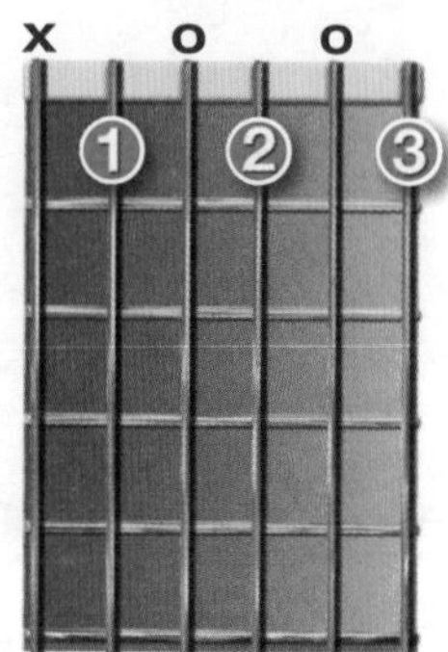

Chord Spelling

1st (B♭), 3rd (D), 5th (F), ♭7th (A♭), ♭9th (C♭)

B♭9$^{\flat 5}$

Dominant 9th Flattened 5th

(1st position)

Chord Spelling

1st (B♭), 3rd (D), ♭5th (F♭), ♭7th (A♭), 9th (C)

B7$^{\sharp 5}$

Dominant 7th Sharpened 5th

(1st position)

Chord Spelling

1st (B), 3rd (D♯), ♯5th (Fx), ♭7th (A)

B7$^{\sharp 9}$

Dominant 7th Sharpened 9th

(1st position)

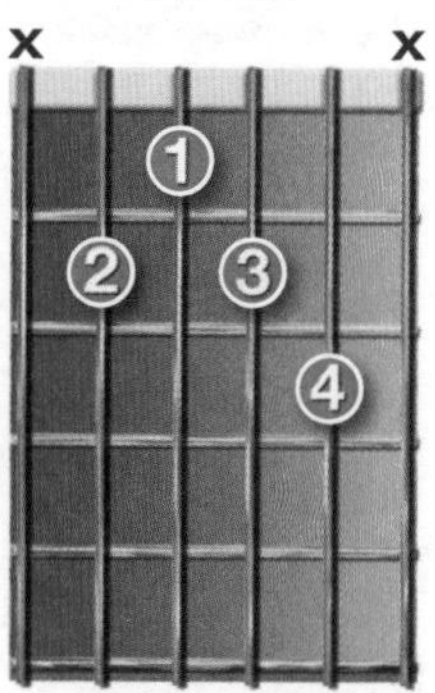

Chord Spelling

1st (B), 3rd (D♯), 5th (F♯), 7th (A), ♯9th (Cx)

B7$^{\flat 5}$

Dominant 7th Flattened 5th

(1st position)

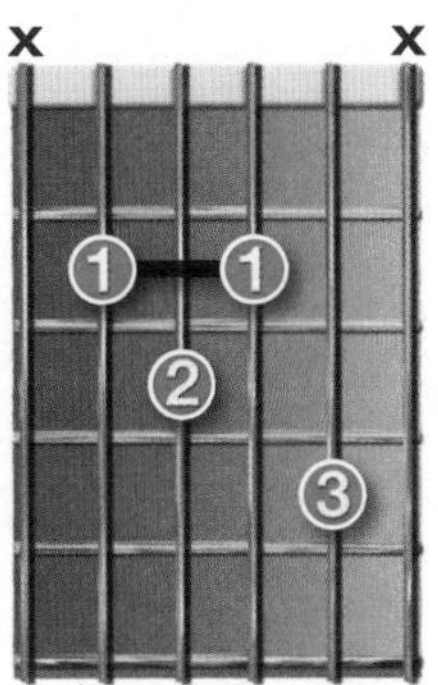

Chord Spelling

1st (B), 3rd (D♯), ♭5th (F), ♭7th (A)

B7$^{\flat 9}$

Dominant 7th Flattened 9th

(1st position)

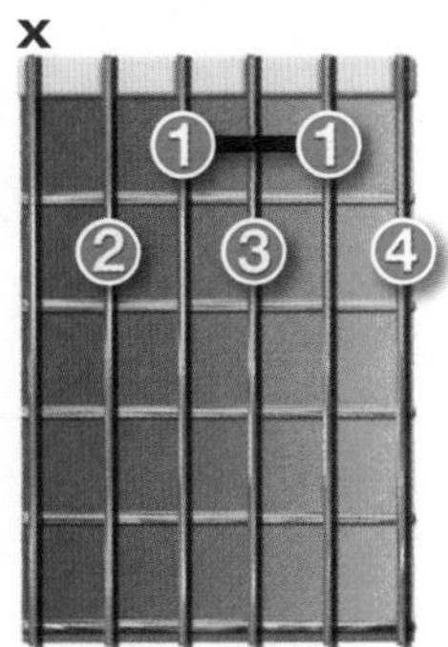

Chord Spelling

1st (B), 3rd (D♯), 5th (F♯), ♭7th (A), ♭9th (C)

B9$^{\flat 5}$

Dominant 9th Flattened 5th

(1st position)

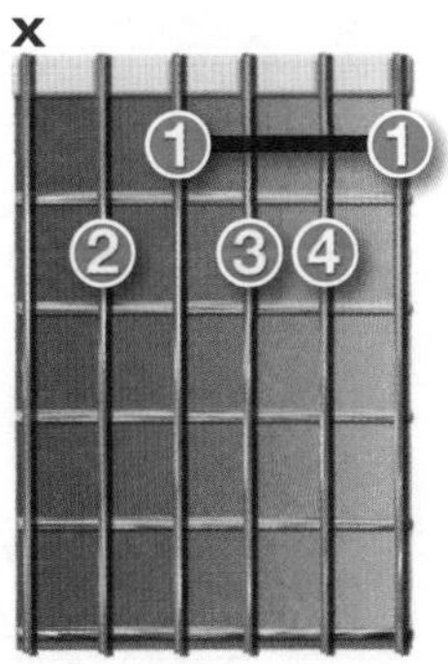

Chord Spelling

1st (B), 3rd (D♯), ♭5th (F), ♭7th (A), 9th (C♯)

C7$^{\sharp 5}$

Dominant 7th Sharpened 5th

(1st position)

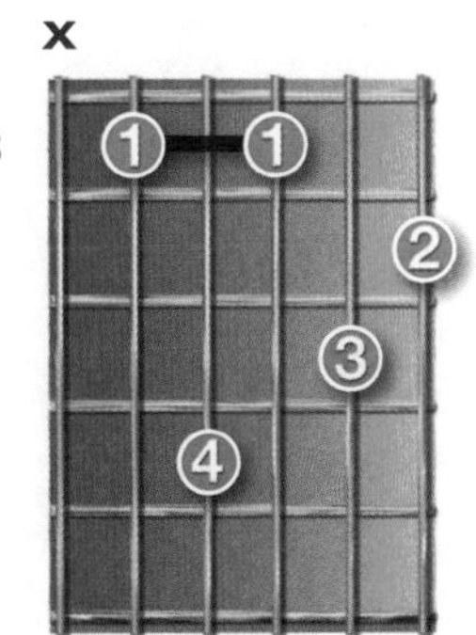

Chord Spelling

1st (C), 3rd (E), ♯5th (G♯), ♭7th (B♭)

A
B♭/A♯
B
C
C♯/D♭
D
E♭/D♯
E
F
F♯/G♭
G
A♭/G♯
Other Chords

C7♯9

Dominant 7th Sharpened 9th

(1st position)

Chord Spelling

1st (C), 3rd (E), 5th (G), ♭7th (B♭), ♯9th (D♯)

C7♭5

Dominant 7th Flattened 5th

(1st position)

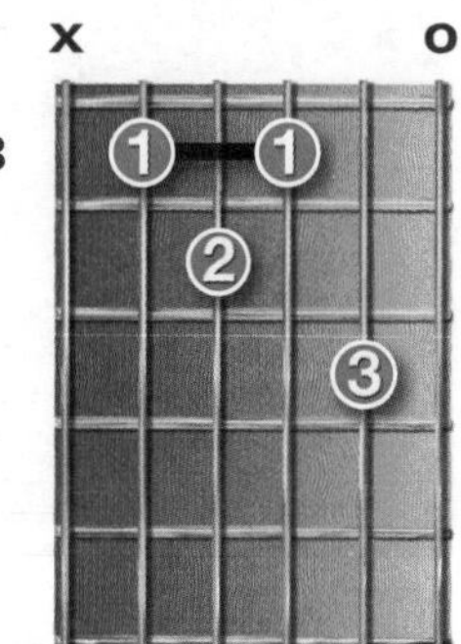

Chord Spelling

1st (C), 3rd (E), ♭5th (G♭), ♭7th (B♭)

C7♭9

Dominant 7th Flattened 9th

(1st position)

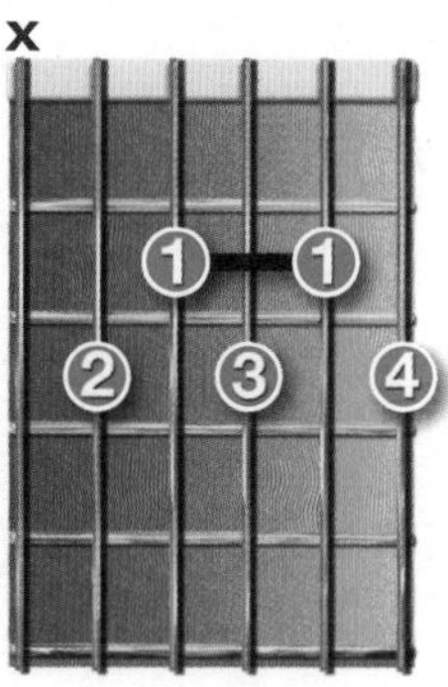

Chord Spelling

1st (C), 3rd (E), 5th (G), ♭7th (B♭), ♭9th (D♭)

C9♭5

Dominant 9th Flattened 5th

(1st position)

Chord Spelling

1st (C), 3rd (E), ♭5th (G♭), ♭7th (B♭), 9th (D)

C♯7♯5

Dominant 7th Sharpened 5th

(1st position)

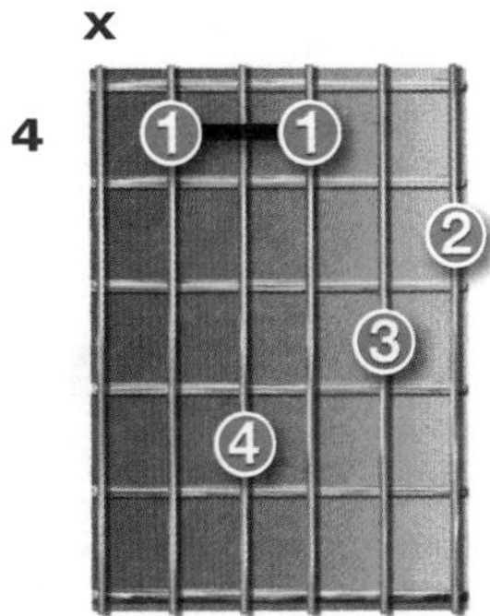

Chord Spelling

1st (C♯), 3rd (E♯), ♯5th (Gx), ♭7th (B)

C♯7♯9

Dominant 7th Sharpened 9th

(1st position)

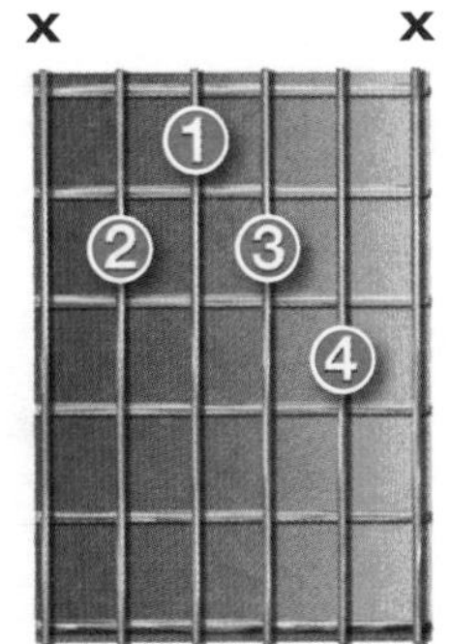

Chord Spelling

1st (C♯), 3rd (E♯), 5th (G♯), ♭7th (B), ♯9th (Dx)

C♯7♭5

Dominant 7th Flattened 5th

(1st position)

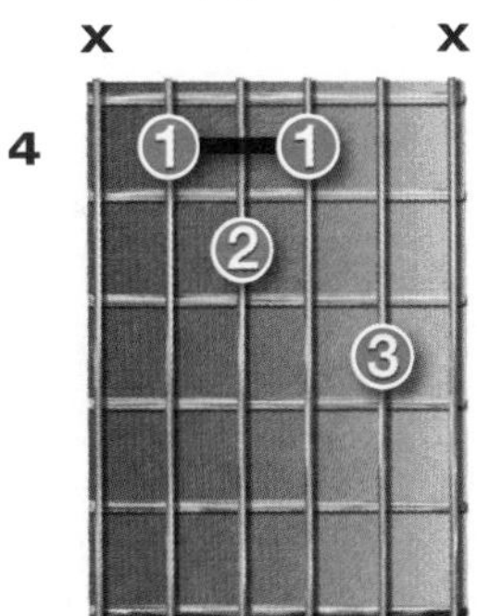

Chord Spelling

1st (C♯), 3rd (E♯), ♭5th (G), ♭7th (B)

C♯7♭9

Dominant 7th Flattened 9th

(1st position)

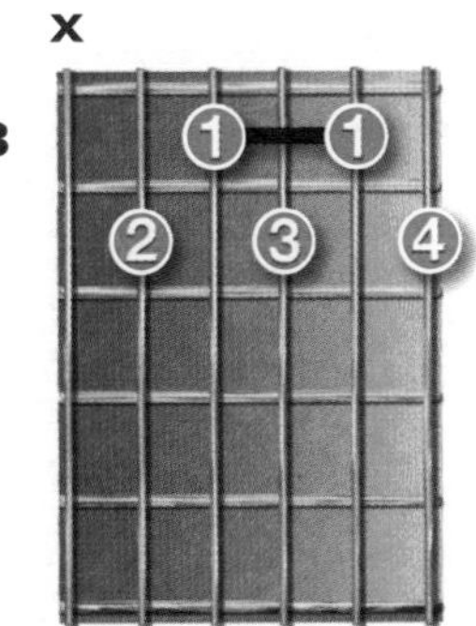

Chord Spelling

1st (C♯), 3rd (E♯), 5th (G♯), ♭7th (B), ♭9th (D)

C♯9♭5

Dominant 9th Flattened 5th

(1st position)

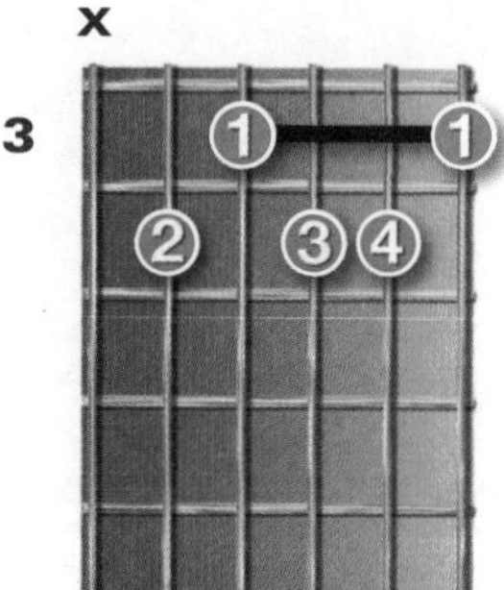

Chord Spelling

1st (C♯), 3rd (E♯), ♭5th (G), ♭7th (B), 9th (D♯)

D7♯5

Dominant 7th Sharpened 5th

(1st position)

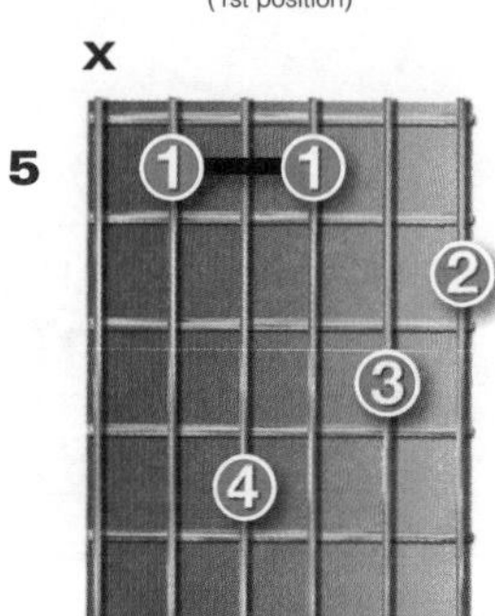

Chord Spelling

1st (D), 3rd (F♯), ♯5th (A♯), ♭7th (C)

D7♯9

Dominant 7th Sharpened 9th

(1st position)

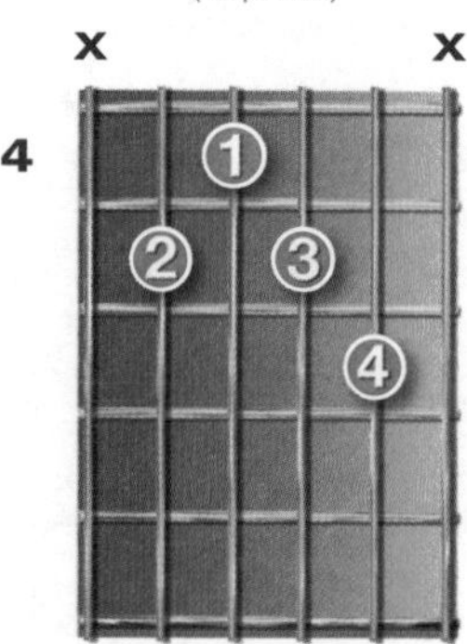

Chord Spelling

1st (D), 3rd (F♯), 5th (A), ♭7th (C), ♯9th (E♯)

D7♭5

Dominant 7th Flattened 5th

(1st position)

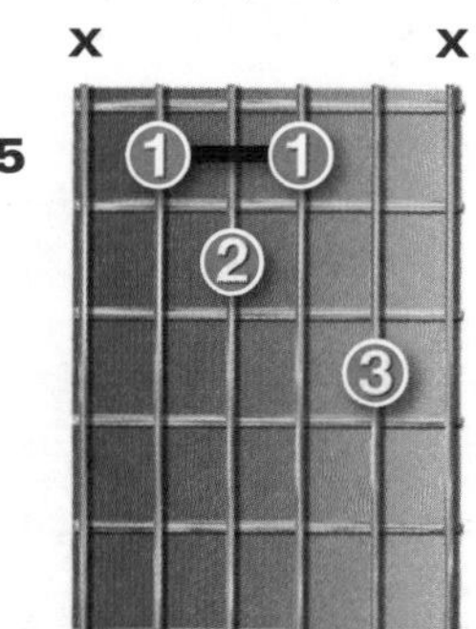

Chord Spelling

1st (D), 3rd (F♯), ♭5th (A♭), ♭7th (C)

D7♭9

Dominant 7th Flattened 9th

(1st position)

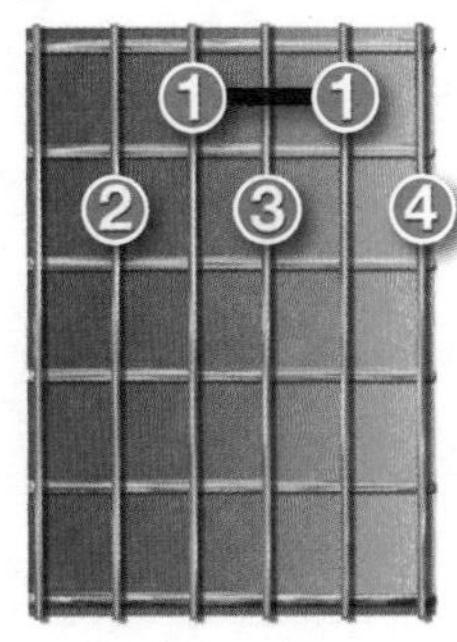

Chord Spelling

1st (D), 3rd (F♯), 5th (A), ♭7th (C), ♭9th (E♭)

D9♭5

Dominant 9th Flattened 5th

(1st position)

4

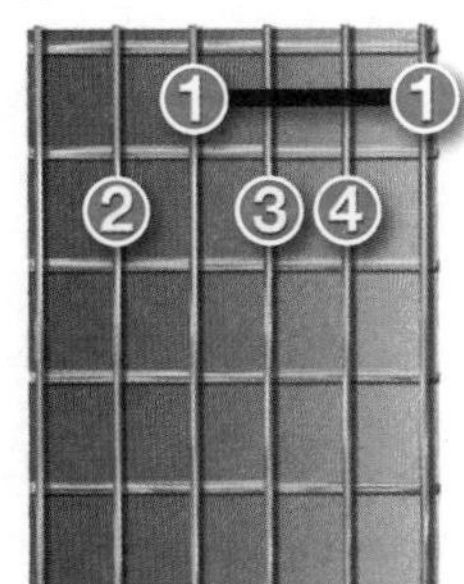

Chord Spelling

1st (D), 3rd (F♯), ♭5th (A♭), ♭7th (C), 9th (E)

E♭7♯5

Dominant 7th Sharpened 5th

(1st position)

X

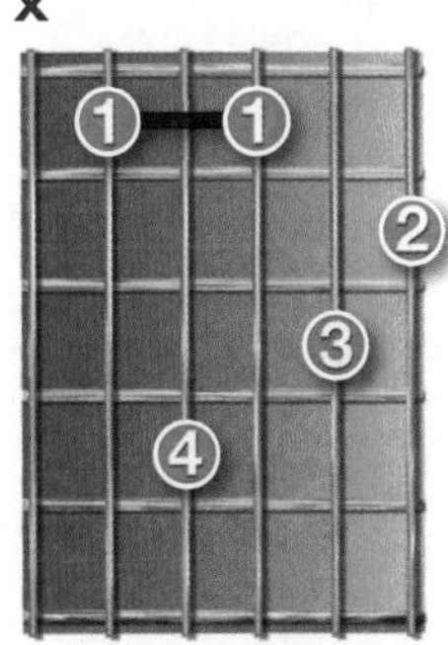

Chord Spelling

1st (E♭), 3rd (G), ♯5th (B), ♭7th (D♭)

E♭7♯9

Dominant 7th Sharpened 9th

(1st position)

X X O

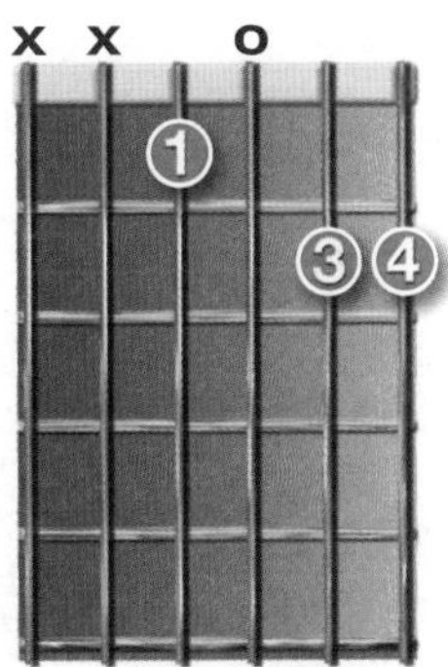

Chord Spelling

1st (E♭), 3rd (G), 5th (B♭), ♭7th (D♭), ♯9th (F♯)

A

D

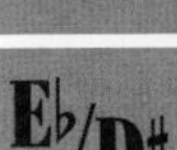

Other Chords

E♭7$^{\flat 5}$

Dominant 7th Flattened 5th

(1st position)

X X
6
1 1
2
3

Chord Spelling

1st (E♭), 3rd (G), ♭5th (B♭♭), ♭7th (D♭)

E♭7$^{\flat 9}$

Dominant 7th Flattened 9th

(1st position)

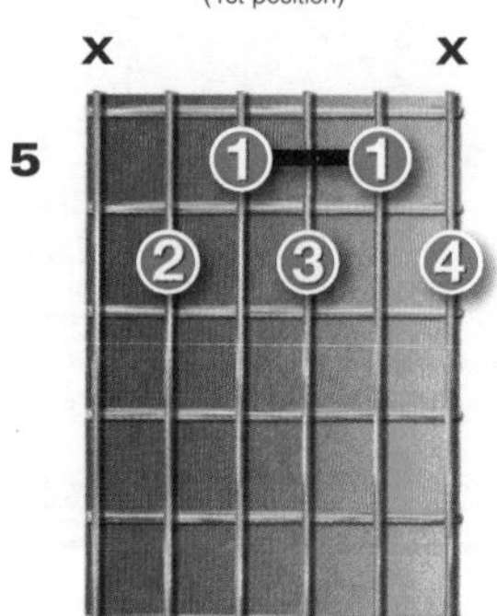

Chord Spelling

1st (E♭), 3rd (G), 5th (B♭), ♭7th (D♭), ♭9th (F♭)

E♭9$^{\flat 5}$

Dominant 9th Flattened 5th

(1st position)

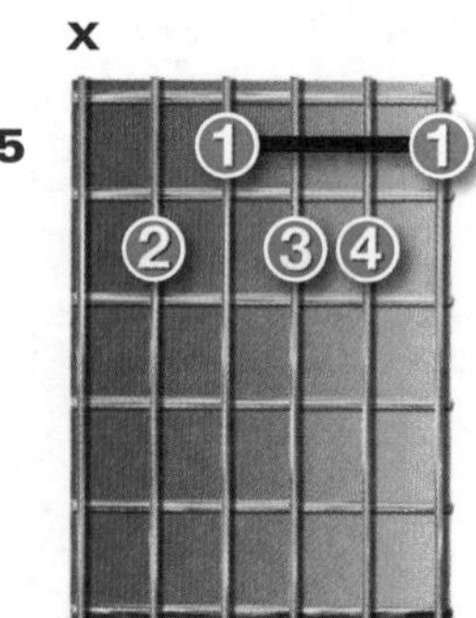

Chord Spelling

1st (E♭), 3rd (G), ♭5th (B♭♭), ♭7th (D♭), 9th (F)

E7$^{\sharp 5}$

Dominant 7th Sharpened 5th

(1st position)

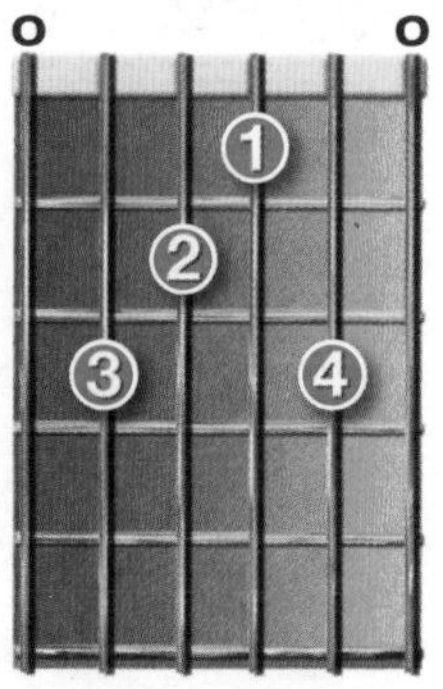

Chord Spelling

1st (E), 3rd (G♯), ♯5th (B♯), ♭7th (D)

$E7^{\sharp 9}$

Dominant 7th Sharpened 9th

(1st position)

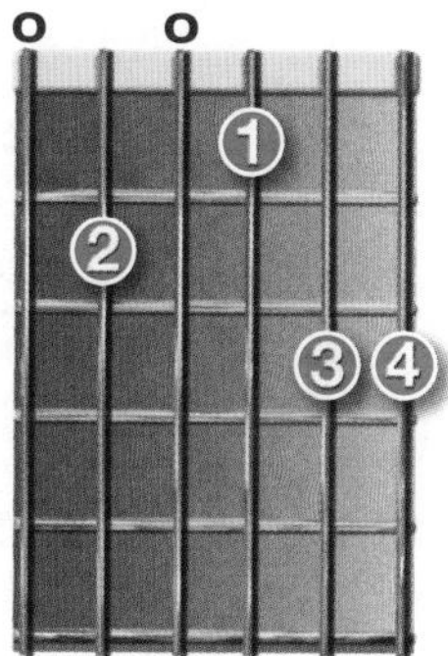

Chord Spelling

1st (E), 3rd (G♯), 5th (B), ♭7th (D), ♯9th (Fx)

$E7^{\flat 5}$

Dominant 7th Flattened 5th

(1st position)

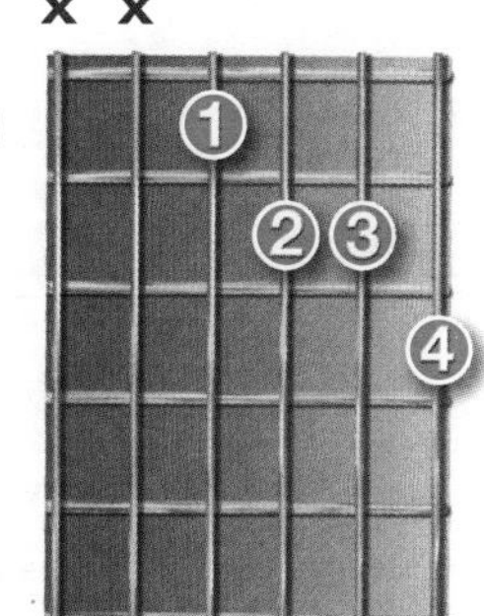

Chord Spelling

1st (E), 3rd (G♯), ♭5th (B♭), ♭7th (D)

$E7^{\flat 9}$

Dominant 7th Flattened 9th

(1st position)

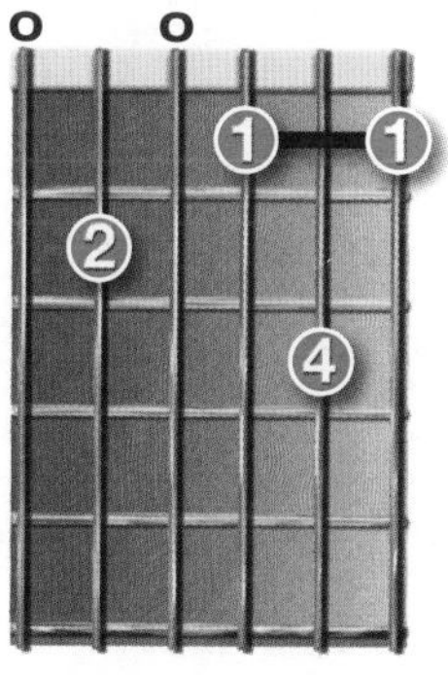

Chord Spelling

1st (E), 3rd (G♯), 5th (B), ♭7th (D), ♭9th (F)

$E9^{\flat 5}$

Dominant 9th Flattened 5th

(1st position)

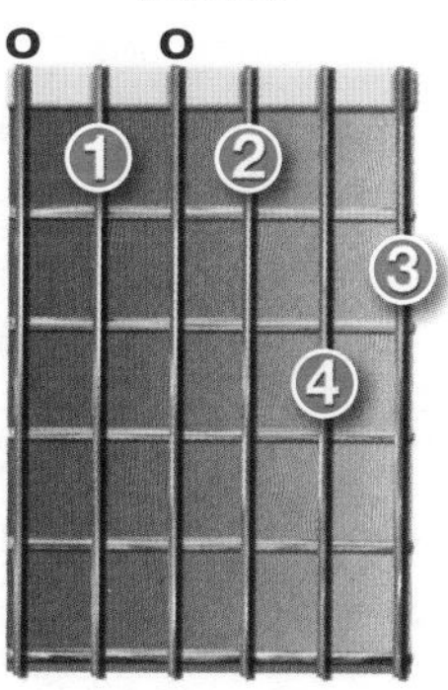

Chord Spelling

1st (E), 3rd (G♯), ♭5th (B♭), ♭7th (D), 9th (F♯)

F7♯5

Dominant 7th Sharpened 5th

(1st position)

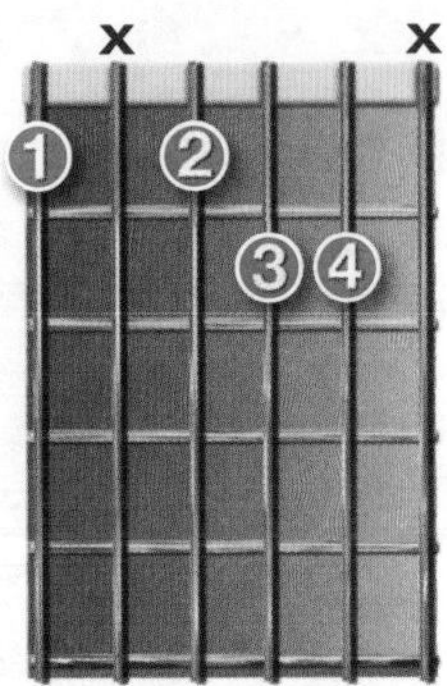

Chord Spelling

1st (F), 3rd (A), ♯5th (C♯), ♭7th (E♭)

F7♯9

Dominant 7th Sharpened 9th

(1st position)

Chord Spelling

1st (F), 3rd (A), 5th (C), ♭7th (E♭), ♯9th (G♯)

F7♭5

Dominant 7th Flattened 5th

(1st position)

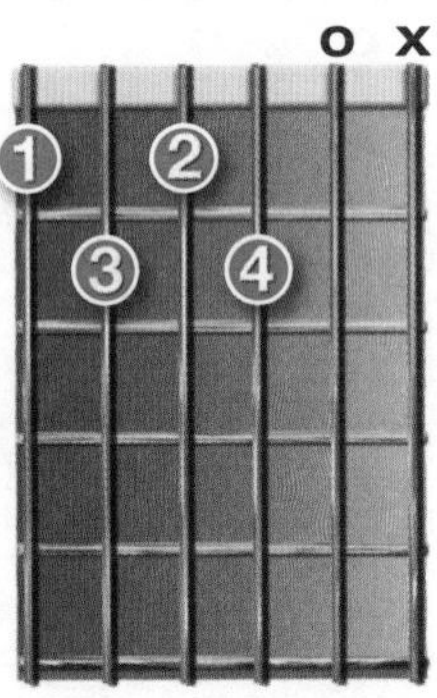

Chord Spelling

1st (F), 3rd (A), ♭5th (C♭), ♭7th (E♭)

F7♭9

Dominant 7th Flattened 9th

(1st position)

Chord Spelling

1st (F), 3rd (A), 5th (C), ♭7th (E♭), ♭9th (G♭)

F9♭5

Dominant 9th Flattened 5th

(1st position)

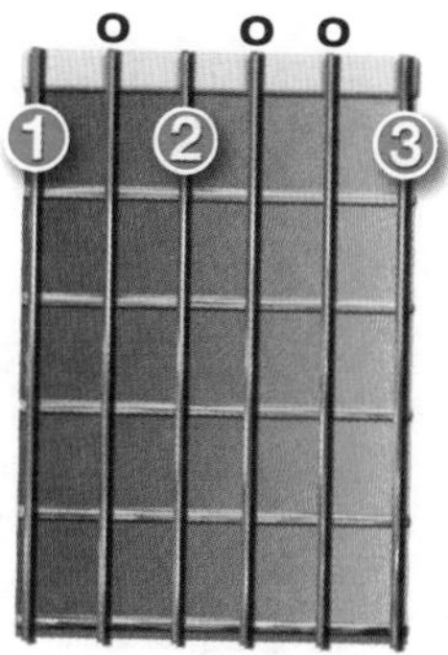

Chord Spelling

1st (F), 3rd (A), ♭5th (C♭), ♭7th (E♭), 9th (G)

F♯7♯5

Dominant 7th Sharpened 5th

(1st position)

Chord Spelling

1st (F♯), 3rd (A♯), ♯5th (Cx), ♭7th (E)

F♯7♯9

Dominant 7th Sharpened 9th

(1st position)

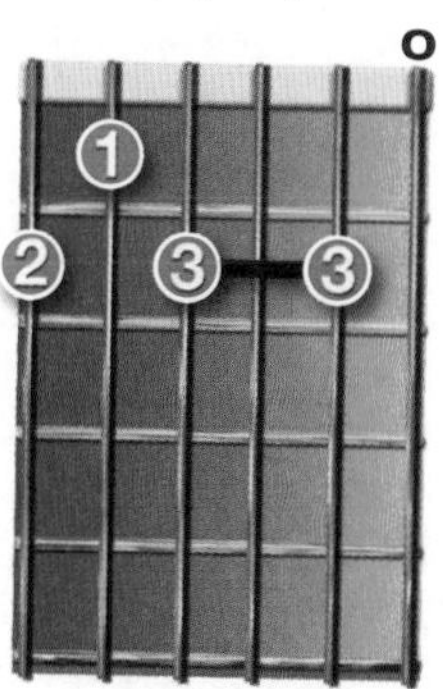

Chord Spelling

1st (F♯), 3rd (A♯), 5th (C♯), ♭7th (E), ♯9th (Gx)

F♯7♭5

Dominant 7th Flattened 5th

(1st position)

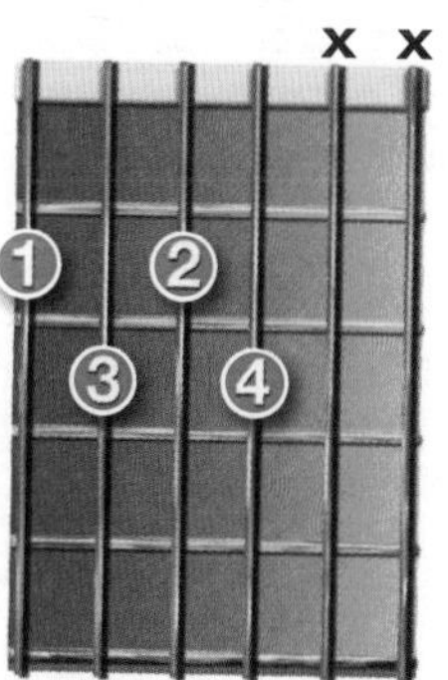

Chord Spelling

1st (F♯), 3rd (A♯), ♭5th (C), ♭7th (E)

F♯7♭9

Dominant 7th Flattened 9th

(1st position)

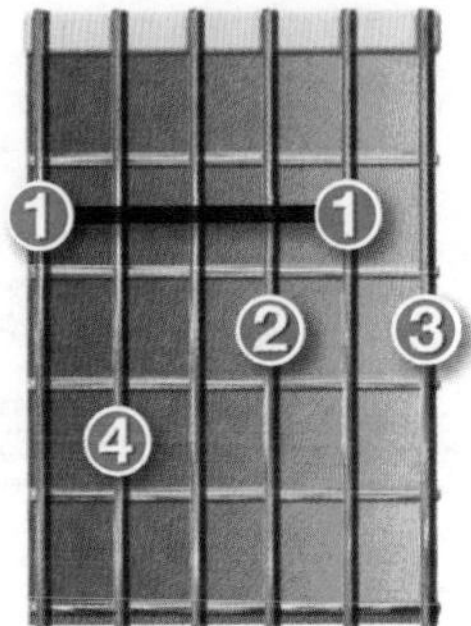

Chord Spelling

1st (F♯), 3rd (A♯), 5th (C♯), ♭7th (E), ♭9th (G)

F♯9♭5

Dominant 9th Flattened 5th

(1st position)

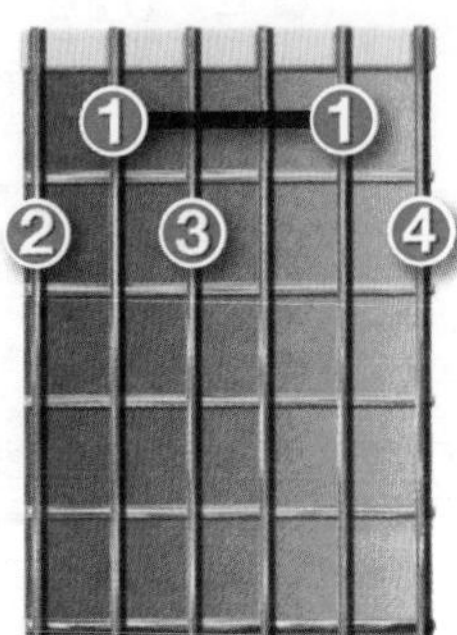

Chord Spelling

1st (F♯), 3rd (A♯), ♭5th (C), ♭7th (E), 9th (G♯)

G7♯5

Dominant 7th Sharpened 5th

(1st position)

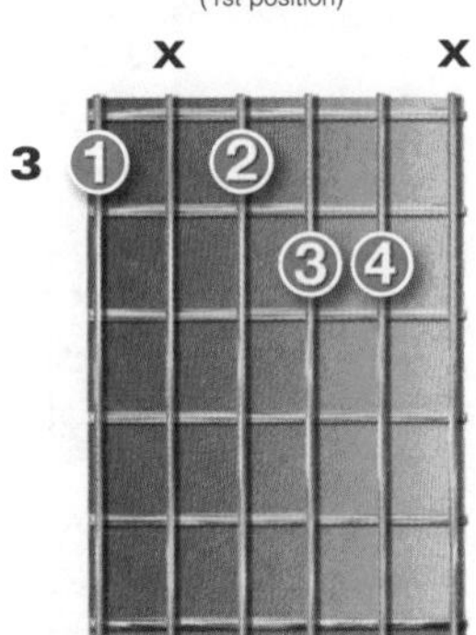

Chord Spelling

1st (G), 3rd (B), ♯5th (D♯), ♭7th (F)

G7♯9

Dominant 7th Sharpened 9th

(1st position)

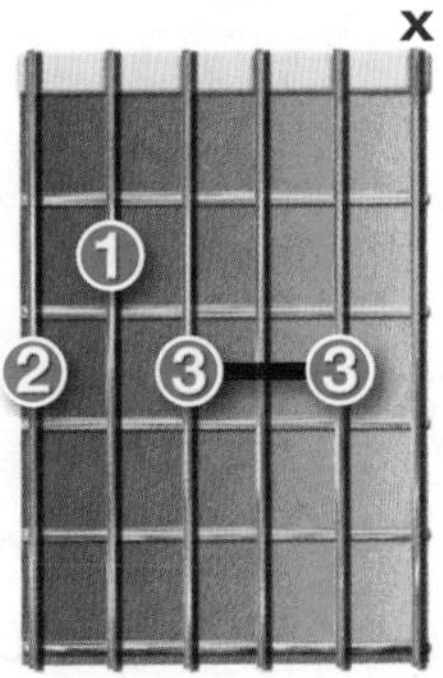

Chord Spelling

1st (G), 3rd (B), 5th (D), ♭7th (F), ♯9th (A♯)

G7♭5

Dominant 7th Flattened 5th

(1st position)

Chord Spelling

1st (G), 3rd (B), ♭5th (D♭), ♭7th (F)

G7♭9

Dominant 7th Flattened 9th

(1st position)

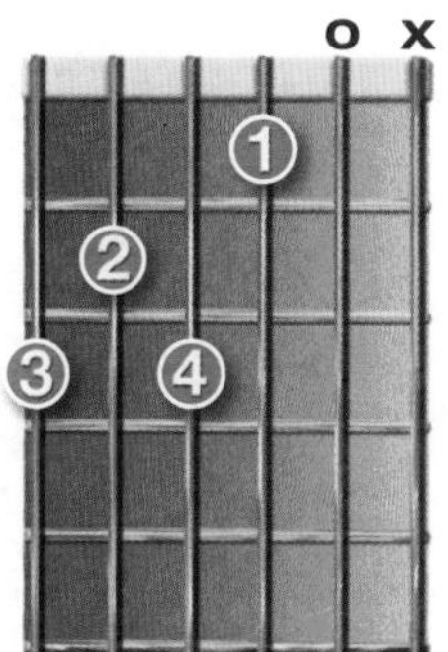

Chord Spelling

1st (G), 3rd (B), 5th (D), ♭7th (F), ♭9th (A♭)

G9♭5

Dominant 9th Flattened 5th

(1st position)

Chord Spelling

1st (G), 3rd (B), ♭5th (D♭), ♭7th (F), 9th (A)

A♭7♯5

Dominant 7th Sharpened 5th

(1st position)

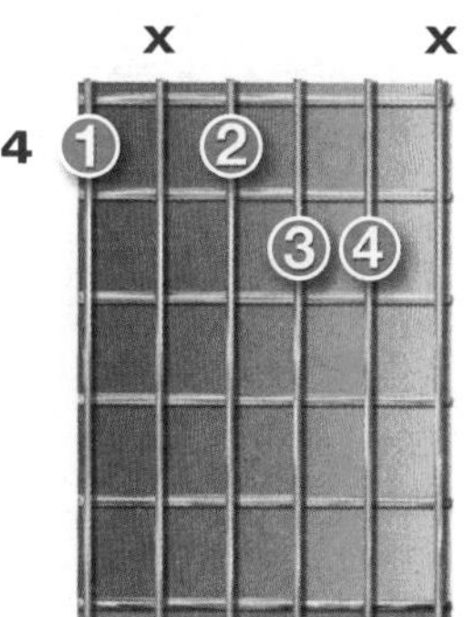

Chord Spelling

1st (A♭), 3rd (C), ♯5th (E), 7th (?)

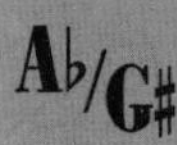

Other Chords

A♭7$^{\sharp 9}$

Dominant 7th Sharpened 9th

(1st position)

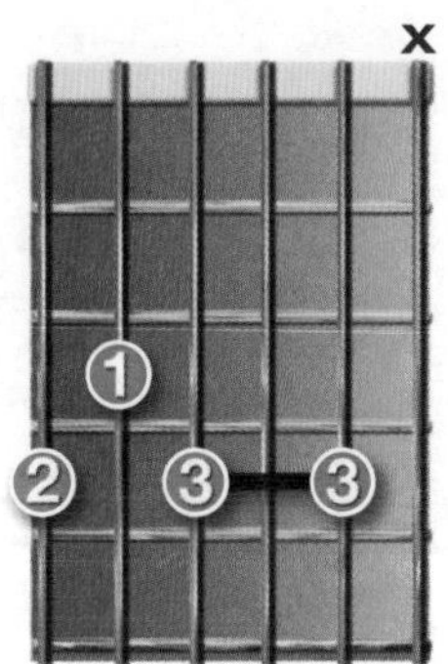

Chord Spelling

1st (A♭), 3rd (C), 5th (E♭), ♭7th (G♭), ♯9th (B)

A♭7$^{\flat 5}$

Dominant 7th Flattened 5th

(1st position)

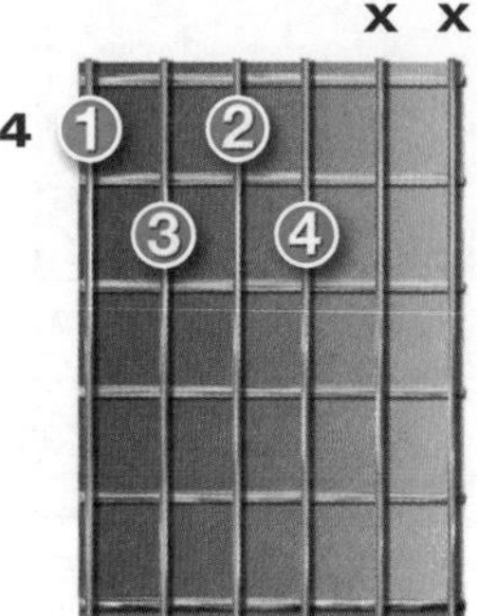

Chord Spelling

1st (A♭), 3rd (C), ♭5th (E♭♭), ♭7th (G♭)

A♭7$^{\flat 9}$

Dominant 7th Flattened 9th

(1st position)

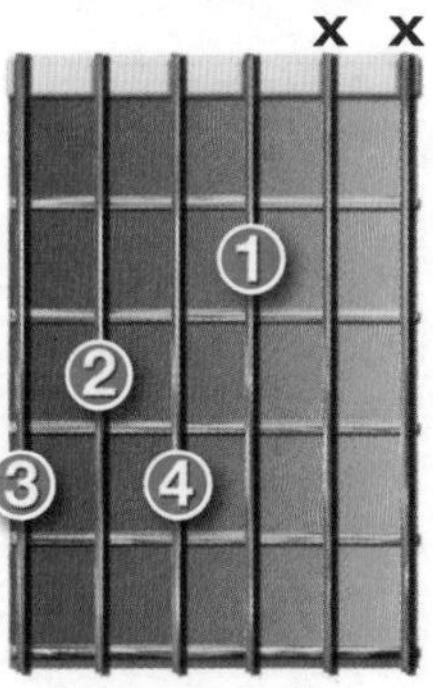

Chord Spelling

1st (A♭), 3rd (C), 5th (E♭), ♭7th (G♭), ♭9th (B♭♭)

A♭9$^{\flat 5}$

Dominant 9th Flattened 5th

(1st position)

Chord Spelling

1st (A♭), 3rd (C), ♭5th (E♭♭), ♭7th (G♭), 9th (B♭)

Some Notes About Chords

Triads

Triads are basic three-note chords that are also the building blocks of all other chords. There are four basic triads: a major triad is the first, third and fifth notes of the diatonic major scale (C, E and G in the key of C); a minor triad is the first, third and fifth notes of the natural minor scale (C, Eb and G in the key of C); an augmented triad is a major triad with a sharpened fifth note (C, E and GI in the key of C); and a diminished triad is a minor triad with a flattened fifth note (C, Eb and Gb in the key of C). All of these basic chords can be extended; a major seventh chord, for example, is a major triad with a seventh note added (C, E, G and B in the key of C).

Open Chords

These are chords in which open strings are used as part of the chord. They are normally, but not exclusively, played at the nut end of the fretboard. They are more often used in acoustic rather than electric guitar playing.

Barre Chords

These are chords in which no open strings are played – instead the first finger lies flat across all the strings. Barre chord shapes are just open-position chords re-fingered, thereby leaving the first finger free for holding the barre. The advantage of barre chords is that once you have learned one shape, you can use it for all of the 12 different keys simply by moving it up or down the neck to change the pitch. This can be especially useful when playing rhythm guitar.

As barre chords do not involve open strings they can sound great with distortion, and are well suited for use with punchy rhythmic techniques (like staccato). The most common barre chords are the 'E' and 'A' shapes based on the E and A open chords respectively. When playing a barre chord, ensure that the first finger is close to, and in line with, the fret rather than at an angle to it.

Further Reading and other useful internet resources for this book are available on **www.flametreemusic.com**

Guitar Chords is another in our best-selling series of easy-to-use music books designed for players of all abilities and ages. Created for musicians by musicians, these books offer a quick and practical resource for those playing on their own or with a band. They work equally well for the rock and indie musician as they do for the jazz, folk, country, blues or classical enthusiast.

FlameTreeMusic.com

Flame Tree Music offers useful, practical information on chords, scales, riffs, rhymes and instruments through a growing combination of traditional print books and ebooks.

Books in the series:

Advanced Guitar Chords; Beginner's Guide to Reading Music; Piano & Keyboard Chords; Chords for Kids; Play Flamenco; How to Play Guitar; How to Play Bass Guitar; How to Play Piano; How to Play Classic Riffs; Songwriter's Rhyming Dictionary; How to Become a Star; How to Read Music; How to Write Great Songs; How to Play Rock Rhythm, Riffs & Lead; How to Play Hard, Metal & Nu Rock; How to Make Music on the Web; My First Recorder Music; Piano Sheet Music; Brass & Wind Sheet Music; Scales & Modes.

For further information on these titles please visit our trading website: www.flametreepublishing.com